D0856722

STEPFAMILIES

GARLAND REFERENCE LIBRARY
OF SOCIAL SCIENCE
(VOL. 317)

STEPFAMILIES
A Guide to the
Sources and Resources

Ellen J. Gruber Ph.D., J.D.

GARLAND PUBLISHING, INC. • NEW YORK & LONDON
1986

Library of Congress Cataloging-in-Publication Data

Gruber, Ellen J.
  Stepfamilies : a guide to the sources and resources.

  (Garland reference library of social science ;
vol. 317)
  Includes index.
  1. Stepfamilies—United States—Bibliography.
I. Title. II. Series: Garland reference library of
social science ; v. 317.
Z7164.M2G78 1986   016.3068'7   85-23111
[HQ759.92]
ISBN 0-8240-8688-0

Printed on acid-free, 250-year-life paper
Manufactured in the United States of America

CONTENTS

INTRODUCTION

One of the oldest living institutions is the family, but the traditional family system is having little success today. The American family has been undergoing great change.

Mother and father experience problems in the relationship as husband and wife. This naturally affects their children. There is anxiety in everyone involved in the troubled situation. The family breaks up. More anxiety and uncertainty prevails. Divorce is at an all time high. The number of divorces has tripled in just two decades and usually there are children involved in the divorces. The very high rate of remarriage, however, indicates that people still believe in marriage. For many, it means a second (or third) chance to make a satisfying life for oneself.

The natural result of the breakdown of the original family is the eventual formation of the stepfamily. Four out of five divorcees will remarry, and one in every four marriages today involves formerly married people.

Fifty million Americans are part of stepfamilies; one out of every six children under eighteen is a stepchild; and each year five hundred thousand adults become stepparents. It is an overwhelming situation, one that demands new information and techniques in order to successfully deal with the enormous complexities. Until recently, there has been a dearth of information on the topic of stepfamilies. Divorce received some attention, but stepfamilies were literally overlooked as a viable topic of concern. This is changing now as evidenced by the entries in this book.

This bibliography attempts to bridge the interchange gap among professionals from different disciplines or between professionals working with children and those working with adults. This bibliography brings together voluminous articles and books from many different disciplines and suggests the various professional and lay audiences for which they are relevant.

Works Cited

This bibliography of books, magazines and journals
will serve as a helpful reference guide to research and
service programs for those in the helping professions who
work with children and families in stepfamily situations.
Books and articles were written from 1980 through 1984.
A few references from an earlier period have been included
because of the uniqueness of an idea. A few dissertations
on the subject of stepfamilies were included because of
the contribution of the authors to the area but generally
dissertations were not focused upon because of their in-
accessibility to the general public. Although availabilit
to the public was a criterion for inclusion in the bibliog
raphy, it was later decided to include up-to-date referenc
which were pertinent but unavailable. Several citations,
therefore, have no annotation but are considered applicabl
Perhaps they will be located in a library in the reader's
locale. It is almost impossible for libraries to have
every work on a particular topic.

It is important to note that limited research studies
have been executed in the area of stepfamilies. Our under
standing of these limited studies as with all research
should be read carefully to interpret the validity of its
results. The research is presented but its validity is
not discussed.

The articles not based on research may offer a review
of literature or a discussion of successful clinical strat

Original exerpts from the abstracts have sometimes
been used in the annotations.

Organization

The major portion of this reference book is a general
bibliographic list, alphabetized by the author's name,
which includes books and articles directed toward professionals who work with children and parents.

The books listed in the general bibliography are primarily useful for professionals such as teachers, day care workers, pediatric nurses, clergy, youth workers, and mental health counselors and psychologists who work with children and adults. Legal and medical professionals such as pediatricians, obstetricians and psychiatrists will find many entries informative.

The major bibliography is supplemented by an extensive bibliography for parents and a bibliography for young children and teenagers.

Following is a list of audio-visual materials available on stepfamilies, and a resource list of organizations for stepfamilies. Newsletters are also provided.

The author is grateful to many interested West Georgia College graduate students who helped research the area of stepfamilies. Extensive research was done by Lee Gruber, the author's daughter and a medical student, who is particularly interested in the topic.

THE BIBLIOGRAPHY

1. Adams, Jay E. *Marriage, Divorce and Remarriage.*
    Grand Rapids, Mich.: Baker Books, 1981.

2. Ahrons, C. "The Continuing Coparental Relationship
    Between Divorced Spouses." *American Journal of
    Orthopsychiatry* 51 (3: 1981): 415-28.

3. Ahrons, Constance R., and Morton S. Perlmutter.
    "Therapy with Remarriage Families: III. The
    Relationship Between Former Spouses: A Sub-
    system in the Remarriage Family." *Family
    Therapy Collections* 2 (1982): 31-46.

    The authors laid groundwork for the centrality
    of the former spouse relationship in the remarriage
    relationship. Their findings assume that a continuing
    relationship between former spouses is necessary
    if they are to successfully coparent their minor
    children. They concur that remarried families are
    in need of education to assist them in constructively
    reorganizing their family.

4. Albert, Linda. *Linda Albert's Advice for Coping
    With Kids.* New York: E.P. Dutton, 1982.

    Written by the Director of the Family Education
    Center of Florida, this book is a comprehensive

collection of practical solutions to everyday
problems parents face. Divorce and remarriage
are addressed.

5. Albrecht, Stan L., and Howard M. Bahr. *Divorce*
    and Remarriage: Problems, Adaptations and
    Adjustments. Westport, Conn.: Greenwood, 1983.

6. Asmundsson, Rigmor. "Blended Families: One Plus
    One Equals More Than Two." *Understanding the*
    Family: Stress and Change in American Family
    Life. Edited by Cathleen Getty and Winifred
    Humphreys. New York: Appleton-Century-Crofts,
    1981.

7. Atwell, Anthony, E., Ursula S. Moore, and Carla S.
    Nowell. "The Role of Stepparents in Child
    Custody Disputes." *Bulletin of the American*
    Academy of Psychology and the Law 10 (March 1982):
    211-17.

    This article explores the roles and relationships
    of stepparents with their current spouses, with
    both ex-spouses, with their children, and with
    their stepchildren, during the time of custody and
    visitation disputes. Both positive and negative
    motivations are explored and two cases are presented
    to illustrate the stepparent role in such disputes.

8. Auerbach, Sylvia. "Stepping into Grandparenting."
    Psychology Today 17 (4: April 1983): 56-57.

    Instant grandparents! What is it like to become
    an instant grandparent? (In other words, an instant
    stepgrandparent.) There are many organizations
    to help stepfamilies but there are no resources
    for stepgrandparents. From a survey of parents
    whose children were marrying someone with children
    the answers were the same: anxiety and apprehension,
    strongly influenced by concern about the choice of
    a mate. Many stages of coming to grips with your
    role are at hand: guilt; anger; new concerns; and
    first meeting. For those who want the special bond

that can exist between grandparents and grandchildren, it can be cultivated and be especially
sweet because it is one of choice.

9. Bachrach, Christine A. "Children in Families:
   Characteristics of Biological, Step and Adopted
   Children." *Journal of Marriage and the Family*
   45 (1: February 1983): 171-9.

   This article presents the characteristics of
   children living with biological mothers, stepmothers
   and adoptive mothers and the various relationships
   that exist between the child, the mother, and the
   father. Most information suggested that children
   living with both biological parents had similar
   characteristics to those living with a biological
   parent and a stepparent. The children who did not
   have a father figure present in the home were
   generally poorer, especially if the mother had never
   been married. Economically, adopted children were
   more advantaged than children living with stepparents
   or biological parents.

10. Baden, Clifford, ed. *Parenting After Divorce*.
    Boston: Wheelock College, 1981. 48 pp.

    In seven brief presentations, social attitudes
    toward divorce, experiences and problems families
    face after divorce and the phenomenon of mini-
    families within the stepfamily are discussed.
    The minifamily is a concept used to describe
    learned social behaviors from past family settings
    that affect the new stepfamily.

11. Baptiste, David A., Jr. "Marital and Family Therapy
    With Racially/Culturally Intermarried Stepfamilies:
    Issues and Guidelines." *Family Relations* 33 (3:
    1984): 373-80.

    Discusses difficulties experienced by intermarried
    stepfamilies. Author seeks sensitivity from mental
    health professionals to the issues specific for
    treating such families.

12. ———. "Masks as a Therapeutic Modality in
      Reduction of Role Stress in Reconstituted
      Families." Paper presented at the annual meeting
      of the National Council on Family Relations,
      Portland, Oregon, October 1980.

13. Berger, R. *Stepchild*. New York: Simon and
      Schuster, 1980.

14. Berger, Stuart. *Divorce Without Victims: Helping
      Children Through Divorce with a Minimum of
      Pain and Trauma*. Boston: Houghton Mifflin, 1983.

      A psychiatrist's complete guide for parents who
      need help with children during divorce. The book
      explains how to honestly answer children's questions
      about divorce. The author shows parents how to
      recognize children's emotional problems and how
      children hide their problems.

      Attention is also given to remarriage and the
      complex relationships of the stepfamily. A
      chapter is included on when and where to seek help.

15. Bergguist, Beatrice. "The Remarried Family: An
      Annotated Bibliography, 1979-82." *Family
      Process* 23 (March 1984): 107-19.

      The focus of this reference-oriented article
      is on the remarried family and the characteristics
      common to its formation and integration. It is
      divided into six sections: (1) demography/legal
      issues; (2) remarriage as a transition; (3) re-
      marriage formation, restructuring relationships;
      (4) children in remarried families; (5) treatment
      issues, and (6) how-to books. Very complete
      annotations.

16. Berman, Claire. "The Instant Parent." *Redbook*
      157 (1: May 1981): 119, 168, 170, 172.

The author tells many of the things she learned through interviews she conducted, while working on a four year project to identify and understand the special problems of reconstituted families. She finds common areas of concern, and learns how these families are coping with remarriage.

17. ————. *Making It as a Stepparent: New Roles New Rules*. New York: Doubleday, 1980.

Berman uses hundreds of interviews with remarried men and women to examine remarriage and almost exhausts the topic. She discusses many issues that play a significant role in stepfamilies, i.e., money, sex and discipline, as well as giving information about support groups.

18. ————. *What Am I Doing in a Stepfamily?* Secaucus, N.J.: Lyle Stuart, 1982.

With compassion and humor this charmingly illustrated book touches on the issues relevant to the young stepchild, including the most important question, "Where do I fit in?" Its candid look at the sensitive issues involved in the breakup and reconstitution of families helps grownups and reassures the child that he or she is loved.

19. Berman, E. *The New-Fashioned Parent: How to Make Your Family Style Work*. Englewood Cliffs, N.J.: Prentice-Hall, 1980.

This book provides guidelines for traditional families, stepfamilies and single-parent families.

20. Bernstein, Barton E., and Berna G. Haberman. "Lawyer and Counselors as an Interdisciplinary Team: Problem Awareness in the Blended Family." *Child Welfare* 60 (April 1981): 211-18.

Blended families which consist of a newly married couple, their children by former marriages
and their children by this marriage, are becoming
more common on the American scene. This creates
both legal and counseling problems. This article
suggests that couples entering into a complex
marriage situation consider a premarital agreement to protect themselves, their property and
their children. A counselor can help with sibling
rivalry and other parenting issues that are often
similar to those of the nuclear family, the major
difference being the merging of two unique families.

21. Bohannan, Paul. *Bibliography*. Towson, Maryland:
    Stepfamily Association of America, Inc., 1983.

    A partially annotated bibliography of books,
    journal articles, dissertations, etc., relating
    to stepfamilies. Particularly helpful for
    students and researchers. Updated at regular
    intervals.

22. Bohham, Sharon Price, and Jack O. Balswick. "The
    Noninstitutions: Divorce, Desertion and Re-
    marriage." *Journal of Marriage and the
    Family* 42 (4: November 1980): 959-72.

    This article is a review of the literature and
    research published in the 1970's dealing with
    divorce, desertion and remarriage. Suggested
    in this review is the idea that divorce and
    remarriage are beginning to develop patterns of
    regularity moving toward institutionalization.
    Discussed are such topics as divorce and the
    necessary adjustments to be made, mate selection
    in the process of remarriage, marital happiness,
    adjustment problems for reconstituted families
    and desertion. At this point, little research
    has been completed which deals with desertion.
    In order for greater success in dealing with
    these situations, more research needs to be
    provided and more support systems made available.

23. Bowerman, Charles E. "Some Relationships of
    Stepchildren to Their Parents." *Journal of
    Marriage and the Family* 24 (1982): 113-28.

    This study attempted to find associations
    among children's feelings of closeness to
    their parents. It tested the general hypothesis
    that the relationship of children with the father
    is a more reliable index of family integration
    than is the children's relationship with the
    mother and that the relationship of children
    with both parents is an even more accurate index
    of family integration. The study supports pre-
    vious research in that it found closeness of
    children to either the mother or the father to be
    associated with positive values, behavior and
    self-evaluations.

24. Bridgwater, Carol Austin. "Second Marriages
    Fare Better with Childless Husbands."
    Psychology Today 16 (March 1982): 18.

    This article cites the results of a survey of
    married couples by W. Glenn Clingempeel, Department
    of Psychology, Temple University. The purpose of
    the survey was to determine marital satisfaction
    in remarriages which involve both simple and
    complex stepfamilies. The conclusion is that if
    the wife has children, the partners' marital
    satisfaction is likely to be higher if the man
    does not have children.

25. Brooks, Jane B. *The Process of Parenting*.
    Palo Alto, Calif.: Mayfield Publishers, 1981.

    This book presents information on physical,
    intellectual, social and emotional growth from
    birth to adolescence.

    Parents need a variety of techniques for
    handling situations with children, depending on
    the specific characteristics of the child and
    the problem. To provide a range of techniques,

the book describes five strategies of parenting
and shows how they are applied to particular
problems. Three strategies emphasize communicating feelings and establishing relationships with
children. Two strategies emphasize ways of
changing behavior. Parents can find solutions
in these different approaches if they adopt a
problem-solving method that consists of defining
the problem, thinking about alternative actions,
taking action, evaluating the results and sometimes
starting over.

26.   Burgess, R.L., J.A. Kurland, and J.L. Lightcap.
      "Child Abuse: A Test of Some Predictions From
      Evolutionary Theory." *Ethology and Sociobiology*
      3 (2: 1982): 61-67.

      This article confirms findings that within a
      household it is the stepparent-stepchild relation-
      ship that is more likely to be abusive. Findings
      also indicated that males are more likely than
      females to be abusive. Nonevolutionary models that
      rely upon social and psychological factors as
      determinants of abuse do not predict discriminatory
      child abuse. Abuse of one child within a home would
      place all other children in the home at risk. In
      this sense, the evolutionary model of parental
      behavior makes a unique prediction about the kinds
      of parental care. Moreover, the nonevolutionary
      models of child abuse fail to account for the male
      bias among abusers and victims.

27.   Capon, Robert Farrar. *A Second Day: Reflections
      on Remarriage.* New York: Morrow, 1980.

      The author, an Episcopal minister, addressed
      the hope implicit in remarriage. He suggests
      letting go of the unchangeable past which is an
      ongoing death in us. Although he has personally
      experienced marriage, divorce and remarriage,
      he has fictionalized the characters in the book.
      A religious book.

28. Cate, Rodney M. "Reconstructed Families."
    Christian Singles 5 (10: January 1984): 38-39.

    The author suggests how an individual or couple
    can go about preventing problems that might arise
    in a reconstituted family and presents some guide-
    lines for dealing with child rearing in recon-
    stituted families, a major problem mentioned by
    stepparents.

29. Cauhape, Elizabeth. *Fresh Starts--Men and Women
    After Divorce.* New York: Basic Books, Inc., 1983.

    This book represents the first scientific account
    of the effects of divorce at mid-life, examining
    the opportunities for growth as well as the problems
    that must be solved. Stepfamilies are discussed
    briefly.

30. Cherlin, Andrew K. *Marriage, Divorce, Remarriage.*
    Cambridge, Mass.: Harvard University Press, 1981.

    Cherlin looks at the marital trends through
    research on marriage, divorce, and remarriage
    since World War II. He presents the facts and
    examines the reasons for the changes in our
    society. Excellent graphs are provided as a
    study of the statistics.

31. Chillman, C. "Remarriage and Stepfamilies:
    Research Results and Implications." In E.D.
    Macklin and R.H. Rubin (eds.), *Contemporary
    Families and Alternative Lifestyles*. Beverly
    Hills, Calif.: Sage, 1983.

32. Clausen, Peggy, William Burger, Pamela Abramson,
    John McCormic, and Sandra Cavazos. "Divorce
    American Style: Grandparents' Rights."
    Newsweek (January 10, 1983): 47-48.

    Grandparents have followed in the footsteps of
    unhappy divorced fathers; they became a single
    interest group. Forty-two states now give grand-
    parents the right to go to court and demand to see

their grandchildren. Five years ago these laws
were unheard of, but due to the upheavals in family
patterns they are more common. Mix and match marriages have in the past left grandparents out in
the cold.

33. Clingempeel, W. Glenn. "Quasi-kin Relationships
     and Marital Quality." *Journal of Personality
     and Social Psychology* 41 (5: 1981): 890-901.

     In this article the author tests the hypothesis
     that the relative instability of remarriages is due
     to the absence of societal role prescriptions to
     regulate steprelationships with quasi-kin, i.e.,
     former spouses, their blood relatives, and the
     people they remarry. Couples in the study were
     divided into three levels of frequency of contact
     with quasi-kin groups (high, moderate, and low).
     Those with moderate levels of contact with quasi-
     kin were found to exhibit better marital quality.

34. Clingempeel, W. Glenn, Eulalee Brand, and Richard
     Ievoli. "Stepparent-Stepchild Relationships in
     Stepmother and Stepfather Families: A Multi-
     method Study." *Family Relations* (33: 1984):
     465-73.

     Examines characteristics of stepparent-stepchild
     relationships in stepmother and stepfather families.
     Findings show stepparent-stepdaughter relationships
     in both stepmother and stepfather families were more
     problematic than stepparent-stepson relationships.

35. Coleman, C. "The Effects of Structural Variables
     on Spousal Consensus in Remarried Couples."
     Unpublished master's thesis. Washington State
     University, 1981.

36. Coleman, Marilyn, and Lawrence H. Ganong. "Effect
     of Family Structure on Family Attitudes and
     Expectations." *Family Relations* 33 (3: 1984):
     425-32.

The authors examine the effects of family structure and family integration on children's attitudes toward marriage, marriage roles and divorce as well as the effects of cause of marital disruption, type of stepfamily, length of time in the stepfamily and family integration on step-children's attitudes toward marriage, marriage roles and divorce.

37. Coleman, Marilyn, Lawrence H. Ganong, and Jane Henry. "What Teachers Should Know About Step-families." *Childhood Education* 60 (May/June 1984): 306-9.

The authors begin by mentioning several step-family stereotypes found in fairy tales and real life and then explain how schools seemed to have neglected the reality of stepfamilies. The authors enumerate specific suggestions for raising teacher awareness about stepfamilies.

38. Colvin, B.D. "Adolescent Perceptions of Intra-familial Stress in Stepfamilies." Ph.D. dissertation. Florida State University, 1981.

39. Colvin, B.D., M.W. Hicks, and B.B. Greenwood. "Intrafamilial Stress in Stepfamilies: Research Findings and Theoretical Implications." Paper presented at National Council on Family Relations. Milwaukee, Wis., 1981.

40. Cottle, Thomas J. *Children's Secrets*. Garden City, N.Y.: Anchor Press, 1980.

This book is a collection of a psychologist's interviews with children. Children tell their perceptions on parental abandonment, infidelity, physical battering, divorce, remarriage and other family problems. This is an excellent book for counselors who deal with children.

41. "Counseling Families." *Children Today* 9 (November-
     December 1980): 26.

     Describes government publication, *Helping Youth
     and Families of Separation, Divorce, and Remarriage:
     A Program Manual*. Describes three models: family
     counseling model for families experiencing severe
     difficulties; educational model using a structured
     curriculum; and self-help model encouraging
     sharing feelings and information. May be obtained
     free from LSDS, Dept. 76, Washington, D.C. 20401.

42. Crosbie-Burnett, Margaret. "The Centrality of
     the Step Relationship: A Challenge to Family
     Theory and Practice." *Family Relations* 33
     (3: 1984): 459-63.

     Findings show step relationships rather than
     marital relationships significant to overall
     happiness in the family. Discusses implications
     for theory and practice.

43. Currier, Cecile, L.C.S.W. *Learning to Step
     Together*. Towson, Maryland: Stepfamily
     Association of America, 1982.

     A leaders manual for educators and mental
     health practioners leading courses or workshops
     for couples in stepfamilies. Complete with hand-
     out suggestions.

44. Day, R.D., and W.C. Mackey. "Redivorce Following
     Remarriage: A Re-evaluation." *Journal of
     Divorce* 4 (3: 81): 39-47.

45. DeMaris, Alfred. "A Comparison of Remarriages
     with First Marriages on Satisfaction in Marriage
     and its Relationship to Prior Cohabitation."
     Family Relations 33 (3: 1984): 443-49.

     Authors examine marital satisfaction between
     first marriages and remarriages and its relation-
     ship to prior cohabitation. Results showed no
     significant difference in these areas.

46. Dostal, Judy W., and Thomas S. Parish. "Evaluations of Self and Parent Figures by Children from Intact, Divorced, and Reconstituted Families." *Journal of Youth and Adolescence* 9 (1980): 347-51.

    Children from intact families tended to evaluate themselves and their parents more positively than those from divorced families. Children from re-married families, as opposed to children from non-remarried families, were found to evaluate themselves somewhat more positively.

47. Dowling, Claudia. "The Relative Explosion." *Psychology Today* (April 1983): 55-59.

    This article begins by describing the tangled web of relationships that exist today, but which has its roots in the sixties generation. The author also points out that with this relative explosion, the togetherness could be maintained were it not for a housing shortage making it very difficult to live under one roof. Even simple things, like introductions, become complex, the author also points out. Suggestions for coping with other stepfamily issues are also included.

48. Einstein, Elizabeth. *The Stepfamily: Living, Loving, and Learning*. New York: Macmillan Publishing Co., 1982.

    This important book chronicles the developmental passages of the stepfamily through experiences of the author (a stepchild and twice a stepmother), interviews with more than fifty other stepfamilies and discussions with professionals who work with them. This highly readable book won a national media award from the American Psychological Association.

49. Elliot, Karen Sue Brim. "A Study of the Quality
    of Remarriage." Ph.D. dissertation. Kansas
    State University, 1981.

    Author studied the quality of marriage of sixty
    selected remarried couples. Her purpose was to
    survey demographic characteristics related to
    remarriage and to obtain spouses' perceptions of
    joys and difficulties experienced in remarriage.

50. Emery, A. *Stepfamily*. Philadelphia, Pa.:
    Westminister Press, 1980.

    This work of fiction centers around a remarriage
    involving the four Mackey children and the three
    Duncan children. Very realistic portrayal of
    stepfamily life.

51. Englund, C.L. "Parenting and Parentage: Distinct
    Aspects of Children's Importance." *Family
    Relations* 32 (1: January 1983): 21-28.

    Interviews with a childless couple, a couple
    who adopted children, a blended couple, a couple
    who chose to have their own children, a grandparent
    couple, and a great-grandparent couple are presented
    in this article. The interviews were conducted to
    help couples gain insight into why they chose to
    be parents or why they chose not to.

52. Esses, Lillian M., and Richard Campbell.
    "Challenges in Researching the Remarried."
    Family Relations 33 (3: 1984): 415-24.

    Discusses problems for researching stepfamilies.
    Presents practical guidelines and recommendations
    for overcoming common methodological obstacles.

53. Fields, Terri. "Learning to Live with a Step-
    parent." *Seventeen* (April 1983): 97.

    This brief article focuses on teenagers'
    reactions to their parents remarrying, encompassing
    emotions from jealousy to disloyalty to insecurity
    to guilt to relief. A clinical psychologist's

tips for feeling happier and more accepting of
parents remarrying are included. Written in
clear language.

54. Fisch, Richard, John H. Weakland, and Lynn Segal.
    The Tactics of Change. San Francisco, Calif.:
    Jossey-Bass Publishers, 1982.

55. Fishman, B., and B. Hamel. "From Nuclear to
    Stepfamily Ideology: A Stressful Change."
    Alternative Lifestyle 4 (2: 1981): 181-204.

56. Fishman, Barbara. "The Economic Behavior of
    Stepfamilies." *Family Relations* 32 (3: July
    1983): 359-66.

    Economic behavior in this article is used as an
    indicator of a remarried couple's commitment to
    one another and to each other's children. Two
    economic patterns that stepfamilies adopt are
    described: "Common Pot" families pool all their
    resources for household expenses, and "Two Pot"
    couples safeguard individual resources for personal
    use or for their biological children. The author
    suggests that the common pot economy lends itself
    to unifying the stepfamily, whereas the two pot
    economy encourages biological loyalties and
    personal autonomy.

57. Formanek, Ruth, and Anita Gurian. *Why? Children's
    Questions, What They Mean and How to Answer Them*.
    Boston: Houghton Mifflin, 1980.

    Two psychologists discuss how to give appropriate
    answers to difficult questions, according to child's
    age. The chapter on remarriage is of particular
    interest. Questions on parent and child relation-
    ships and child rearing are explored.

58. Fowler, Rod. "Efficacious Factors for Facilitating
    the Emotional Adjustment of Children in Re-
    marriage." *Psychology, A Quarterly Journal of
    Human Behavior* 18 (2/3: Summer-Fall 1981): 50-53.

Four factors have been identified in this literature as crucial to facilitate the emotional
adjustments of a child in remarriage: (1) the
pre-remarriage adjustment of the child; (2) the
age of the child at the time of remarriage; (3)
the stepparent-stepchild relationship; and (4)
the presence of stepsiblings. A dual-focused,
dual phasic preventative program was presented.

59. Furstenberg, F.F., Jr., and G. Spanier. "Marital
    Dissolution and Generational Ties." Paper
    presented at the biennial meeting of the Society
    for Research in Child Development, Boston, Mass.
    April 1981.

60. Furstenberg, F.F., Jr., G.B. Spanier, and N.
    Rothschild. "Patterns of Parenting in the
    Transition from Divorce to Remarriage." In
    P.W. Berman and E.R. Ramey (eds.), *Women: A
    Developmental Perspective*. Washington, D.C.:
    DHHS (NIH Publ. No. 82-2298), 1982.

61. Furstenberg, Frank F., Jr., and Graham B. Spanier.
    "The Risk of Dissolution in Remarriage: An
    Examination of Cherlin's Hypothesis of Incom-
    plete Institutionalization." *Family Relations*
    33 (3: 1984): 433-41.

    A review of data supporting Cherlin's belief
    that remarriages suffer a high rate of dissolution
    because remarriage is an incomplete institution.
    Authors suggest certain characteristics of
    remarriers and the remarriage process contribute
    to the high rate of divorce in second marriages.

62. Ganong, Lawrence H., and Marilyn Coleman. "The
    Effects of Remarriage on Children: A Review
    of the Empirical Literature." *Family Relations*
    33 (3: 1984): 389-406.

    The authors critically examined and discussed
    the effects of remarriage on children presented
    in thirty-eight empirical studies. They found

little evidence that children in stepfamilies differ from children in other family structures.

63. Garbarino, James, et al. *Families At-Risk for Destructive Parent-Child Relations in Adoles-cence.* Pennsylvania State University: University Park Institute for the Study of Human Development, 1982. (ERIC No. Ed. 227, 393, 36 pages).

This paper examines the parental, adolescent and family system characteristics that place a family at risk for destructive parent-child relations in adolescence.

The results of the research supported the hypoth-esis that the high-risk group tends to be "chaotic" and "enmeshed"; to include more stepparents; to be more punishing and less supportive; and to be more stressed by life changes. Adolescents in the high-risk families have more developmental problems, and the number of such problems correlates significantly with the risk for destructive parent-child relations.

64. Garfield, Robert. "The Decision to Remarry." *Journal of Divorce* 4 (1: 1980): 1-10.

Remarriage is an increasingly common phenomenon that affects millions of men, women and children. A general profile of remarriage and the process by which divorced people decide to remarry is presented. A format is described through which clinicians can evaluate critical issues that determine the readiness of divorced people to remarry.

65. Giles-Sims, Jean, and David Finkelher. "Child Abuse in Stepfamilies." *Family Relations* 33 (3: 1984): 407-13.

Review of data showing relationship between stepparenting and child abuse. Examines five theories: social-evolutionary; normative; stress; selection; resource, which can or have been used to explain the relationship.

66.   Glick, P.C. *Personal Comments: Master Lecture*.
      Lecture presented at the annual meeting of the
      National Council on Family Relations, Washington,
      D.C., 1982.

67.   ———. "Remarriage: Some Recent Changes and
      Variations." *Journal of Family Issues* (1980):
      455-78.

      This article presents data about trends in
      divorce and remarriage, examining more closely the
      rapid rise in divorce that occurred in the 1970's
      and the extent to which various categories of
      divorced persons have remarried. The author also
      interprets probable factors involved in these
      divorce and remarriage phenomena and addresses
      policy implications of the data.

68.   Goetting, Ann. "The Six Stations of Remarriage:
      Developmental Tasks of Remarriage After Divorce."
      Family Relations 3 (1982): 213-22.

      The article consists of an analysis of causal
      explanations for the increasingly common nature of
      remarriage after divorce, as well as a description
      of six developmental tasks faced by persons
      approaching remarriage. This developmental process
      is an extension of Paul Bohannan's six stations of
      divorce and involves the emotional, psychic,
      community, parental, economic and legal stations
      of remarriage.

69.   Goldmeier, John. "Intervention in the Continuum
      from Divorce to Family Reconstitution." *Social
      Casework* 61 (1980): 39-47.

      This article develops a theory for practice
      with families somewhere on the continuum from
      divorce to family dismemberment to family re-
      constitution. Sensitivity to the timing of

intervention and the need to formulate an open-ended treatment contract to maintain client-therapist continuity are suggested. The author identifies three major impediments for coping: guilt, fear and loneliness.

70. Greenwalt, Julie. "Is Second Wife, Second Best? Author Glynnis Walker Explores the Pitfalls of Being Spouse No. 2." *People* 22 (4: July 23, 1984): 75-78.

   This article serves to explore Glynnis Walker's new book, *Second Wife, Second Best?* The author gives candid, yet brief, answers to questions about the stereotypes of second wives, problems, ex-wives, sex, financial matters, advantages and preparing to be a second wife.

71. Grossman, Sharlyn M., Judy A. Shea, and Gerald R. Adams. "Effects of Parental Divorce During Early Childhood on Ego Development and Identity Formation of College Students." *Journal of Divorce* 3 (1980): 263-72.

   Comparisons of family backgrounds: intact, divorced and divorced-remarried of 294 college students failed to show that divorce backgrounds meant lower levels of ego development, identity achievement, or locus of control.

72. Hafkin, Marc I. "Association Factors for Step-father Integration within the Blended Family." Ph.D. dissertation. American University, 1981.

   The premise in this study is that a satisfactory spousal relationship is pivotal for successful stepfather integration. Other variables, i.e., involvement with stepchildren, discipline and financial conflict, are explored as well.

73. Hanes, Helen Chancey. "Perceptions of Family
     Concepts of Stepfather and Stepmother Stepfamily
     Dyads." Ph.D. dissertation. Texas Woman's
     University, 1981.

     This study compared perceptions of family con-
     cepts between natural mother and stepfather and
     natural father and stepmother. It was concluded
     that there were no significant differences between
     these two stepfamily dyads.

74. Hare-Mustin, Rachel. "China's Marriage Law: A
     Model for Family Responsibilities and Relation-
     ships." *Family Process, Inc.* 21 (December 1982):
     477-81.

     A description of the change in the marriage laws
     since 1950 is described. The 1981 law is concerned
     with equality and the lawful needs of women,
     children, and the aged. Family planning is
     encouraged. Divorce is easier to obtain. Adoptees
     and stepchildren are now provided for.

     Article 21 concerns stepchildren. "No maltreat-
     ment or discrimination is allowed between step-
     parents and stepchildren. Relevant provisions of
     the law apply to the rights and duties between
     stepfathers or stepmothers and their stepchildren
     who receive care and education from stepparents."

75. Hepworth, Jeri, G. Robert Ryder, and Albert S.
     Dreyer. "The Effects of Parental Loss on the
     Formation of Intimate Relationships." *Journal
     of Family Therapy* 10 (1: 1984): 73-82.

     The effects of parental loss (through death or
     divorce) on subsequent intimate relationships were
     studied with a sample of young married couples
     and with a sample of college students. Persons
     with parental divorce generally indicated acceler-
     ated courtship patterns, as opposed to avoidance
     of intimacy. Theoretical and clinical implications
     are discussed. In a very broad sense this could
     be related to stepfamilies.

76. Hetherington, M.E., M. Cox, and R. Cox. "Divorce and Remarriage." Paper presented at the annual meeting of the Society for Research in Child Development, Boston, Mass., April 1981.

77. Hocking, David. *Marrying Again--A Guide for Christians*. Old Tappan, N.J.: Fleming H. Revell Company, 1983.

This book is an excellent guide for counselors and parents. Written with biblical teachings and practical advice, it is designed to help divorced people in decision-making regarding their new lives and how to adjust to them.

78. Hunter, James E., and Nancy Schuman. "Chronic Reconstitutions as a Family Style." *Social Work* 25 (6: 1980): 446-51.

The authors see family change as an on-going process, based on the notion that some form of serial monogamy is inevitable in modern life. Hunter and Schuman suggest that the chronic re-constituting family is normal and an appropriate variation of the traditional pattern. They feel these new lifestyles can be free, more creative and, generally, more adaptive to modern society.

79. Ihinger-Tallman, Marilyn, and Kay Pasley. "Concep-tualizing Marital Stability: Remarriage as a Special Case." Paper presented at the annual meeting of the National Council on Family Relations, Portland, Oregon, October 1980.

80. ———. "Factors Influencing Stability in Re-marriage." Paper presented at the XIX I.S.A./ C.F.R. International Seminar on Divorce and Remarriage, Leuven, Belgium, August 1981.

81. Jackson, Michael, and Jessica Jackson. *Your Father's Not Coming Home Anymore*. New York: Richard Marek, 1981.

This book gives the views of a cross-section of divorce victims--the children of divorce.

Thirty-eight interviews of young people are compiled. These interviews contain graphic accounts of real reactions to divorce and its many aspects, such as coping with the divorce itself, stepparents, custody, and the reasons for the divorce.

82. Jacobson, Doris S. "Stepfamilies." *Children Today* 9 (January/February 1980): 2-6.

This article discusses stepfamilies from three viewpoints: what has been learned from researchers about stepfamily life (with special reference to child adjustment and stepfamily interaction), the author's own experiences in leading and coordinating groups of stepparents, and preventive and therapeutic approaches to use in working with stepfamilies. The studies conducted provide no clear or final answer in regard to the well-being of children growing up in a stepfamily situation. Some studies indicate no difference between children in stepfamilies and those raised by two biological parents. Other researchers have reached different conclusions. The author suggests that those embarking on a stepfamily experience should first discuss the issues which are likely to arise, a kind of rehearsal for reality which will allow them to understand and deal more effectively with them.

83. Jensen, Janet M., and Larry C. Jensen. *Stepping into Step Parenting: A Practical Guide.* Palo Alto, Calif.: R and E Research Associates, 1981.

The book first emphasizes the importance of developing realistic perceptions and goals for the new family. After pointing out how to move in a positive direction, an easy-to-use system of family organization is presented. This system is based on providing more positive outcomes and

is followed by a chapter on how to enrich family
life after increased love and trust has had time
to develop. The last section presents solutions
for problems facing stepfamilies today.

84. Johnson, Harriette C. "Working with Stepfamilies:
Principles of Practice." *Social Work* 25:4 (July
1980): 304-8.

Among a variety of alternative family arrangements, so-called reconstituted families that
include stepparents and stepchildren are increasingly prevalent today. Some common characteristics
of stepfamilies include a high degree of complexity
and variability; unexpressed or unformulated role
expectations; competition for resources of time,
money, and affection, often attended by losses
and gains for family members; conflicts related
to turf; and differences in lifestyles. Certain
benefits derived from membership in a reconstituted
family have also been noted.

85. Juroe, David J., and Bonnie B. Juroe. *Successful
Stepparenting.* Old Tappan, N.J.: Fleming H.
Revell, 1983.

Two professional counselors offer a resourceful
collection of guidelines based on their personal
experiences and training as preparation for the
responsibilities and rewards of successful
stepparenting. Their sensitive, informative
advice provides valuable insights. Christian
emphasis.

86. Kargman, Marie Witkin. "The Impact on Stepchildren
When Remarried Parents Divorce." Paper pre-
sented at the annual meeting of the National
Council on Family Relations, Milwaukee, Wis.:
October 1981.

87. ————. "Stepchild Support Obligations of Stepparents." *Family Relations* 32 (2: 1983): 231-8.

The legal responsibilites of support by stepparents for stepchildren during remarriage is
discussed. Implications for the impact of the
divorce upon child support, visitation and custody
after divorce from the remarriage are presented.
Court cases and laws relevant to stepchild support
obligations of stepparents are reviewed. The
article cites recently enacted legislative updates
(as of 2/12/80) for twenty-one states.

88.   Keillor, Garrison. "My Stepmother, Myself."
        The Atlantic 249 (3: March 1982): 77-79.

This article presents the myth of the stepmother
being cruel and wicked and uses three satires on
the stories of Snow White, Hansel and Gretel and
Cinderella to set the record straight on the
real relationship between stepdaughters and
stepmothers. Very creative and funny article.

89.   Kelsey, L.J., G. Nass, and R.M. Sabatelli.
        "Factors Mediating the Response to Divorce:
        A Role Transition Perspective." Paper presented
        at the annual meeting of the National Council
        on Family Relations, Milwaukee, Wis., October
        1981.

90.   Kent, Marilyn O. "Remarriage: A Family Systems
        Perspective." *Social Casework* 61 (3: 1980):
        146-53.

A social systems model provides a framework for
understanding the complex dynamics of remarriage.
The behavior of each family member can be viewed
as an effort to define and maintain boundaries,
to appropriately exchange affective energy, and
to negotiate shared purpose. Pivotal theoretical
concepts included are the family mythology, the
negotiation process, the degree of member autonomy,
and the quality of family affect.

91. Keshet, Jamie Kelem. "From Separation to Step-
    family, a Subsystem Analysis." *Journal of
    Family Issues* 1 (4: December 1980): 517-32.

    Explores the subsystem of relationships within
    the stepfamily. These are: the new couple system;
    the ex-spouse system(s); and the parent-child
    subsystem(s), either custodial or visiting parent.
    Through an analysis of existing subsystems that
    compete for limited resources, stepfamilies can
    acknowledge conflicts between and within sub-
    systems and become more unified by defining
    boundaries.

92. Kezar, E.F. "Crisis Theory Related to Divorce
    and Remarriage." Ph.D. dissertation. University
    of North Carolina at Greenwood, 1980.

93. Kirby, Jonell. "Relationship Building in Second
    Marriages and Merged Families." *Journal for
    Specialists in Group Work* 6 (1981): 35-41.

    The author presents two models to facilitate
    work with individuals dealing with relationship
    problems particularly those involved in second
    marriages or merged families. The two models
    explained in the article are the Family Portraits
    model and the French Family Group Technique. Both
    work to develop awareness of the impact of family
    experiences on expectations, needs and individual
    behavior.

94. Klein, E. "Sexual Aspects in Remarriage."
    Unpublished manuscript. Clarke Institute of
    Psychiatry, 1983.

95. Kleinman, Judith, Elinor Rosenberg, and Mary
    Whiteside. "Common Developmental Tasks in
    Forming Reconstituted Families." *Journal of
    Marital and Family Therapy* 5 (2: 1979): 79-86.

This paper illustrates the authors' view of the
tasks with which families or remarriage frequently
struggle.

96. Knox, David. "Trends in Marriage and the Family--
     The 1980's." *Family Relations* 29 (2: April 1980):
     145-50.

This article presents updated information on
thirty-nine trends in marriage and the family.
Some of the topics discussed are sex roles, love
relationships, mate selection, dual careers and
marriage, sexual fulfillment, planning children,
having children, divorce and the later years.
Professionals, who provide students with information
on marriage and parenthood, would find this article
very valuable. Stepfamilies are not directly
mentioned but the information is useful to those
in a stepfamily situation.

97. Kompara, Diane Reinhart. "Difficulties in the
     Socialization Process of Stepparenting." *Family
     Relations* 29 (1: 1980): 69-73.

The paper examines the stepfamily literature and
highlights the socialization difficulties present
in this adjustment process.

Three acute problem areas in the stepfamily
adjustment are: disciplining the children, adjusting to the habits and personalities of the children
and gaining the acceptance of the children.

Clearing up the ambiguity of cultural norms and
legal definitions and changing social policy are
necessary to provide socialization specifics and
to indicate an acceptance of reconstituted families
as a legitimate family form.

98. Kosinski, Frederick A., Jr. "Improving Relation-
     ships in Stepfamilies." *Elementary School
     Guidance and Counseling* 17 (February 1983):
     200-7.

Examines stepfamilies in an attempt to give
elementary school counselors an understanding of
typical behavior for stepfamilies and the individuals that make them up. Special attention
is given to the roles and expectations of stepfamily members and the establishment of stepfamily
boundaries. Strategies for therapeutic intervention and stepparent education are also
discussed.

99.   Kunz, P.R. "The Impact of Social Setting on
       Remarriage: Age of Husband and Wife." Paper
       presented at XIX I.S.A./C.F.R. International
       Seminar on Divorce and Remarriage, Leuven,
       Belgium, August 1981.

100. Laiken, Deidre S. *Daughters of Divorce: The
       Effects of Parental Divorce on Women's Lives.*
       New York: William Morrow and Company, Inc., 1981.

This author states that there is something
about the term "stepmother" that makes us recoil.
There is something about the reality of a stepmother that makes us uncomfortable. All women
who marry a divorced father with daughters can't
be thoughtless, mean and selfish. These are
women who have entered a relationship that has
no room for the angry, newly acquired daughter.
They are also competing against unconscious
drives, intense loyalties, and the image of the
husband's former wife. Due to the increasing
number of second time around families, it is
important that we understand the complex emotions
that put daughters at odds with their father's
second wife.

101. Lamanna, Mary Ann, and Agnes Reidmaan. *Marriage
       and Families: Making Choices Throughout the
       Life Cycle.* Belmont, Calif.: Wadsworth Publish-
       ing Company, 1981.

A textbook based on up-to-date research from
Canadian studies. Covers topics concerning

financial problems, role ambiguity, stepchild's
hostility, stepmother trap and weekend stepmother.

102. Lamb, Michael E. *Nontraditional Families:
        Parenting and Child Development*. Hillsdale,
        N.J.: Laurence Erlbaum Associates, 1982.

        A review of the effects of nontraditional
        family styles on parental behavior and child
        development. Results are from ongoing studies
        in the United States, Sweden, Israel and Australia.

103. "Learning to Step Together." Towson, Md.: Step-
        family Association of America, Inc., 1984.

        This 95 page manual is a six session course
        for stepfamily adults. Topics include myths
        about stepfamilies, structure and complexity
        of stepfamilies, remarriage preparation, strength-
        ening stepcouple relationships, and strategies
        for stepmother and stepfathers, and helping
        children adjust to stepfamily life.

104. LeShan, Eda. "Stepmothers Aren't Wicked Anymore!"
        Parents (June 1980): 57-61.

        Using illustrations from fairy tales, the
        author presents the misconceptions, myths, and
        realities of stepfamilies. She pays particular
        attention to games played, i.e., testing the
        stepparent, preparation for the new marriage,
        conflict of loyalties and problems with younger
        children. She also offers tips for stepparents
        that will help make the remarriage situation work.

105. Leslie, Jacques. "Stepping In." *The New York
        Times Magazine* (April 15, 1984): 7-8.

        The author, a stepfather himself, tells of his
        own personal experience of assimilating into the
        role of husband and father to his wife and
        stepchildren.

106. Lightcap, Joy L., Jeffrey A. Kurland, and Robert
     L. Burgess. "Child Abuse: A Test of Some
     Predictions from Evolutionary Theory."
     Ethology and Sociobiology 3 (2: December 1982):
     61-66.

     In a study which included twenty-four families
     in which there were forty-one parent-child dyads,
     results showed that stepparents significantly
     abuse their stepchildren more often than their
     own children. Males, whether natural fathers or
     stepfathers, are significantly more likely to be
     child abusers than females. A handicapped child
     is much more likely to be abused than a non-
     handicapped child. Elder children are abused
     more often than the youngest child, but elder
     stepchildren aren't abused more often than
     natural elder children, necessarily. Although
     this study confirms the studies of other research-
     ers, they still only represent weak confirmation
     of the evolutionary model.

107. Lindholm, Byron, and John Touliatos. "Teachers'
     Perception of Behavior Problems in Children
     from Intact, Single-Parent, and Stepparent
     Families." *Psychology in the Schools* 17
     (April 1980): 264-69.

     Studies dealing with the effects of parent
     remarriage on children's mental health have
     revealed mixed findings. Some show a greater
     number of behavior problems while some results
     show no difference. This study compared children
     living with natural parents, single parents and
     stepparents. The results showed that children
     living with both parents had fewer overall
     problems. Children living with their father
     only exhibited more socialized delinquency.
     Children with stepparents had more conduct
     problems in school.

108. Longstreth, Langdon E. "Human Handedness: More
      Evidence for Genetic Involvement." *The Journal
      of Genetic Psychology* 137 (2: December 1980):
      275-83.

      "Handedness Inventory," a questionnaire, was
      completed by 1,500 college students. Because
      parents were described as stepparents and half
      and unrelated siblings were described, this
      study was able to be carried out. The sample
      of young adoptees was too small to use to
      determine if stepparents influenced handedness
      among very small children. In another analysis
      results were the same as a study by Hicks and
      Kinsbourne. They found the father-son sex link-
      age in handedness was greater than father-daughter
      effect. Concerning stepparents and their handed-
      ness affecting their stepchildren, this article
      does not go into any depth at all.

109. Lorimer, Anne, and Philip Feldman. *Remarriage--
      A Guide for Singles, Couples, and Families*.
      Philadelphia, Pa.: Running Press, 1980.

      This book is designed to help people deal with
      the many problems involved in a remarriage. Part
      III of the book is devoted to stepfamilies and
      the dynamics of the relationships among members
      of these families. It presents a series of
      chapters that concentrate on the general themes
      that occur, the common problems that arise, when
      children are involved in a second marriage.

110. Louie, Elaine. "The Newest Extended Family."
      House and Garden 153 (7: July 1981): 16-20.

      In a very easily readable format, this article
      discusses the flawed myths about stepfamilies,
      the confusion about names and roles in step-
      families, rules and discipline and the reality
      of having to share your child.

111. Lutz, Patricia. "The Stepfamily: An Adolescent
      Perspective." *Family Relations* 32 (July 1983):
      367-75.

      The purpose of this study was to investigate
      what adolescents believe to be the stressful
      and nonstressful aspects of stepfamily living.
      One hundred and three adolescents between the ages
      12 and 18 who were living in stepfamilies com-
      prised the sample under investigation. Issues
      pertaining to divided loyalties and discipline
      were perceived to be stressful by the greatest
      number of adolescents, and issues pertaining
      to social attitudes and being a member of two
      households were perceived to be stressful by the
      least number of adolescents. Significant relation-
      ships were found between the subjects' perceived
      level of stress and various demographic data.

112. McGoldrick, Monica, and Elizabeth A. Carter.
      "Forming a Remarried Family." In *The Family
      Life Cycle: A Framework for Family Therapy.*
      Edited by E. Carter and M. McGoldrick. New
      York: Gardner Press, 1980.

113. McInnis, Kathleen M. "Bibliography: Adjunct to
      Traditional Counseling with Children of Step-
      families." *Child Welfare* 61 (March 1982):
      153-59.

      The author in this article suggests the use of
      bibliotherapy as a means of helping stepchildren
      resolve confused family roles. As with any other
      type of therapy, there are limitations and
      precautions in using the bibliotherapeutic approach.
      It appears to be most effective with children who
      are in the habit of reading, who have above-average
      intellectual ability, and who are suffering from
      relatively mild to moderate emotional reactions
      to living in a stepfamily.

114. Manning, Anita. "Stepkids Trip Up Remarriage."
      USA Today (November 21, 1983): 1D.

      The author cites six myths of remarriage as
      indicated by sociologists and repeats that
      "problems with stepchildren cause stepparents
      to seek the help of a professional therapist
      more than any other issue."

115. Manosevitz, Martin. "Problems of American Step-
      families." *USA Today* 109 (February 1981): 8.

      According to Manosevitz, about three-fourths
      of all divorced people remarry within ten years.
      About half of these marry other divorced people.
      These figures mean an almost endless array of
      possible configurations of stepfamilies with
      stepparents, stepsisters and stepbrothers. A
      new stepfamily can expect a rocky period of
      adjustment at first, but if it does not resolve
      its problems, "things can go from rocky to worse."
      Manosevitz sees potential benefit in addressing
      conflicts of the stepfamily even before the
      marriage occurs. Premarriage counseling could
      deal with issues of "breaking the news" to
      children and establishing relationship between
      stepparent and child.

116. Messinger, Lillian. *Remarriage: A Family
      Affair.* New York: Plenum Publishers, 1984.

      A noted pioneer and leading authority in the
      field of family counseling, the author provides
      a detailed fascinating account of her study with
      remarried couples and their families. She
      presents her case studies and analyses with
      sensitivity and understanding.

117. Messinger, Lillian, and Kenneth N. Walker.
      "From Marriage Breakdown to Remarriage:
      Parental Tasks and Therapeutic Guidelines."
      American Journal of Orthopsychiatry 51 (July
      1981): 429-38.

This paper focuses on some of the special needs of families with minor children, in particular, the importance of continuity of parenting and the problems typically encountered in moving from marital disintegration to formation of a new marital bond. Suggestions on remarriage are directed to educational programs that can help prepare couples for remarriage with its poorly defined boundaries and rules.

118. Miller, Mark J., and Soper Barlow. "An Emerging Contingency, the Stepfamily: Review of Literature." *Psychological Reports* 13 (June 1982): 715-22.

A noncritical annotated listing of items in the literature on the stepfather, stepmother, step-child and stepfamily. The article is based on the belief that a review of the literature can provide a great deal of information to the practicing counselor. Annotations are brief. Implications for counseling are delineated.

119. Mills, David M. "A Model for Stepfamily Development." *Family Relations* (33: 1984): 365-72.

Stages include general characteristics, setting goals, parental limit-setting, stepparent bonding and blending family rules. Also discussed were exercises for implementing each stage, the use of short-term couple's groups with educational and counseling components and recommendations for planning intervention programs and future research.

120. ———. "Issues in Remarriage: A Clinical Perspective." Paper presented at the annual meeting of the National Council on Family Relations, Portland, Ore., October, 1980.

121. Mitchell, D.W. "Husband Wife Disagreement in Remarried Families: The Development of a New Inventory." Unpublished master's thesis. Washington State University, 1981.

122. Moore, C.E. "Stepfamilies in Victorian Fiction."
      Looking at Stepfamilies. Conference proceedings
      at North Carolina State University, 1980.

123. Morgan, Ann. "The Development of Stepfamilies:
      An Examination of Change Within the First Two
      Years." Ph.D. dissertation. Texas Tech
      University, 1980.

      The purpose of the present study was to examine
      selected aspects of the initial process of re-
      adjustment in reconstituted families. Results
      indicated that satisfaction and unity decreased
      and conflict and problems increased over time.
      Females were significantly less satisfied as the
      length of time in the remarriage increased.

124. Mulford, Phillippa Greene. "Stepparenting: How
      to Star in a Challenging Role." *Vogue*
      (September 1981): 258-63.

      Mulford tells her personal story about embarking
      on a second marriage with a man who already had
      two children and had had a vasectomy. She
      explains how she grew to understand her role as
      a stepparent, not as a substitute parent, but
      as another adult in her stepchildren's lives
      in an open and sincere manner. She also reveals
      how her relationship with her stepchildren
      developed, from an antagonistic one to one of
      mutual love and respect.

125. Nelson, Margaret, and Gordon K. Nelson. "Problems
      of Equity in the Reconstituted Family: A Social
      Exchange Analysis." *Family Relations* 31 (April
      1982): 223-31.

      The authors apply social exchange principles
      in addressing inherent difficulties of setting
      up a stepfamily. A variety of factors that pose
      obstacles to role adjustments and the maintenance
      of equity among members are discussed. It is
      concluded that the stepfamily can merge as a

developmental unit toward expansion and commitment
if the reconstituting family can establish a basis
of trust, so that attractions are formed freely
by persons within and outside the immediate
household.

126. Norment, Lynn. "Should You Marry Someone With
Children?" *Ebony* 38 (1: November 1982): 101-4.

Using real-life examples and advice from a child
psychiatrist and a family therapist, this article
discusses many factors to be considered before
marrying someone with children.

127. Packard, Vance. *Our Endangered Children: Growing
Up in a Changing World*. Boston: Little, Brown,
and Company, 1983.

A guide to the dilemmas facing young children
today, the reference-style volume examines the
settings in which a child is likely to grow up,
and its impact on the child. Parts 3, 4, and 5
(pages 185-385) are of particular interest to
teachers and counselors and others concerned
with family restructure and its effect on children
and adults.

128. Palmero, E. "Remarriage: Parental Perceptions
of Steprelations with Children and Adolescents."
*Journal of Psychiatric Nursing and Mental Health
Services* (April 1980): 9-13.

129. Papernow, Patricia L. "The Stepfamily Cycle:
An Experimental Model of Stepfamily Development."
Family Relations (33: 1984): 355-63.

The seven stages of development in stepfamilies
described enables stepfamily members to easily
recognize their stage in the cycle. It provides
language and experiences upon which the practi-
tioners can base therapy.

130. ————. "A Phenomenological Study of the Devel-
       opmental Stages of Becoming a Stepparent: A
       Gestalt and Family Systems Approach." Ph.D.
       dissertation. Boston University, 1980.

       Qualitative analysis of in-depth interviews
       with nine stepparents revealed a seven stage
       model of development, the stepping cycle. The
       study describes the themes and variations within
       each stage, the obstacles experienced by subjects
       to movement through the cycle, and the varieties
       of support which facilitated movement.

131. Parish, Thomas S., and Judy W. Dostal. "Relation-
       ships Between Evaluations of Self and Parents
       by Children from Intact and Divorced Families."
       Journal of Psychology 104 (1980): 35-8.

       Extending a previous study by Parish and
       Copeland the authors found that for those children
       experiencing divorce and remarriage within the
       two previous years, 1978-80, there appeared to
       be a rather rapid alignment of the self-concepts
       of the children with their mother and stepfather.

132. Parke, Ross D. *Fathers*. Cambridge, Mass.:
       Harvard University Press, 1981.

       This book provides a frank discussion of
       fathering in its many forms: the divorced
       father, the stepfather, the father surrogate, the
       absent father, the dead father, and the house-
       husband. It sticks to known facts. From the
       facts emerges a view of just how satisfying
       and effective successful fathering can be.

133. Pasley, Kay. "An Overview of Remarriage and
       Stepparenting: A Summary of Findings." Paper
       presented at the annual meeting of the American
       Orthopsychiatric Association, Toronto, Canada,
       1980.

This paper presents the results of empirical studies comparing first marriages and remarriages and effects on children and clinical observations, the weaknesses of these studies, and future research needs in a very straightforward, easily understandable format.

134. ————. "Remarriage: What the Literature Reveals." Paper presented at the annual meeting of the National Council on Family Relations, Portland, Ore., 1980.

135. Pasley, Kay, and Marilyn Thinger-Tallman. "Remarried Family Life: Supports and Constraints." *Building Family Strengths IV.* Edited by G. Rowe. Lincoln, Neb.: University of Nebraska Press, 1982.

136. ————. "Stress in Remarried Families." *Family Perspective* 16 (4: 1982): 181-90.

This article offers a conceptualization to help identify stress related problems and to assess the degree of stress encountered in various types of remarried families. It discusses the merging of different family cultures and the establishment of a new family identity, differing perceptions of the rules for distributing family resources and feelings of loyalty to previous and present family members. Recommendations for persons working with remarried families are also offered.

137. Pasley, Kay, Marilyn Thinger-Tallman, and Cathy Coleman. "Consensus Styles Among Happy and Unhappy Remarried Couples." *Family Relations* (33: 1984): 451-57.

Study attempts to describe more clearly the possible styles of agreement among remarried couples. Significant difference between happy and unhappy remarried couples in their perceptions of frequency of agreement or disagreement on family issues.

138. Phillips, Carolyn E. *Our Family Got a Stepparent*.
      Ventura, Calif.: Regal Books, 1981.

      A book with a Christian emphasis for children
      who find themselves in families where, through
      death or divorce, there is a stepparent in their
      lives. Discusses issues chosen in an attempt
      to broaden understanding of children's common
      fears about stepparents and stepfamilies.

139. Pill, C.J. "A Family Life Education Group for
      Working with Stepparents." *Social Caseworker*
      62 (3: 1981): 159-66.

140. Pino, Christopher. *Divorce, Remarriage and
      Blended Families: Divorce Counseling and
      Research*. Palo Alto, Calif.: R and E Research
      Association, 1982.

141. Porterfield, Kay Marie. "Surviving and Thriving
      with Your Stepparent." *Seventeen* (October 1981):
      166-67, 178, 180.

      In a very upbeat manner, the author touches on
      many issues pertinent to being a teenager in a
      stepfamily. Real-life situations are used to
      illustrate points, and tips are provided for
      easing tension in stepfamilies.

142. Price-Bonham, Sharon, and Jack O. Balswick.
      "The Noninstitutions: Divorce, Desertion,
      and Remarriage." *Journal of Marriage and
      the Family* 42 (November 1980): 959-72.

      The article presents data confirming some
      previous findings of research published in the
      1970's on divorce, remarriage and desertion.
      Suggestions for research in the 1980's are
      included. The following topics are discussed:
      demographic and interpersonal nature of divorce;
      adjustment to divorce; remarriage; mate selection;
      marital happiness; adjustment problems for re-
      constituted families; and reasons for desertion
      by males and females.

143. Prosen, Selina Sue, and Jay H. Farmer. "Under-
     standing Stepfamilies: Issues and Implications
     for Counselors." *Personnel and Guidance
     Journal* 60 (March 1982): 393-97.

     The focus of this article is on the children.
     Where are they? What are they feeling? What are
     they doing? How can they be helped and supported?
     The structural and cultural aspects of stepfamilies,
     the effects of stepfamilies on the behavior of
     children, the identification of problem behaviors,
     and intervention strategies are all examined in
     a very readable and informative manner.

144. Radomisli, Michael. "Stereotypes, Stepmothers,
     and Splitting." *American Journal of Psycho-
     analysis* 41 (1981): 121-27.

     The author discusses the wicked stepmother
     stereotype and looks at the psychoanalytic
     phenomenon of splitting in children's fairy
     tales. Splitting refers to the dualism in the
     child of "good mother" and "bad mother."
     Maturation ideally brings about fusion into
     a realistic whole object.

145. Rankin, Joseph. "The Family Context of
     Delinquency." *Social Problems* 30 (4: April
     1983): 466-79.

     Examined in this article is the relationship
     that exists between broken homes and the rate
     of delinquency. Generally, children in broken home
     situations have a higher rate of running away and
     truancy. This type of conduct is affected by
     whether one or both biological parents is absent
     and whether a stepparent is present in the home.
     It did not seem significant in the study of delin-
     quency which parent was absent from the home, nor
     did the cause of separation have a noticable ef-
     fect. This article holds to the assumption, sup-
     ported by research, that a direct relationship

does exist between juvenile misconduct (particularly running away, truancy, and auto theft) and broken homes. Such misconduct was more pronounced in
homes in which both biological parents were missing.

146. Reed, B. *Stepfamilies: Living in Christian
      Harmony.* St. Louis, Mo.: Concordia, 1980.

      This book is based on the author's own experi-
      ences as well as interviews with stepfamilies,
      counselors, pastors and educators. It contains
      discussion questions, case histories, enrichment
      exercises, and a "where to go for help" appendix
      which lists organizations and their addresses.

147. "Remarriage: Special Issue." *Journal of Family
      Issues* 1 (4: December 1980).

148. Rhodes, Sonya, and Josleen Wilson. *Surviving
      Family Life.* New York: G.P. Putnam's Sons, 1981.

      A book written to help people deal with the
      contemporary redefinition of the family unit to
      include communal, single-parented, and extended
      structures. It is a guide to making relationships
      satisfying and rewarding. It deals with the
      blended family and its complex family form.

149. Ricci, Isolina. *Mom's House/Dad's House.* New
      York: Macmillan, 1980.

      A practical and systematic guide to how parents
      can develop a working relationship after a divorce.
      It is based on eight years of research in divorce,
      custody and single parenting. It contains a
      chapter on remarriage and stepfamilies. This
      chapter deals with standards for personal terri-
      tory, discipline, chores and the need for personal
      attention. Each chapter offers specific action
      oriented activities including self-surveys,
      checklists and suggestions.

150. Roberts, C.L. "Building a Developmental Theory: A Propositional Inventory About Stepfamily Transitions." Paper presented at the annual meeting of the National Council on Family Relations Preconference Theory Construction and Research Methodology Workshop. 1980.

151. Roberts, Francis. "Stepfamilies: Stresses and Surprises." *Parents* 56 (March 1981): 108.

    Stepparents, stepchildren and half siblings become more common everyday. Studies show that these families are basically the same as a normal family and that the belief that there are harmful effects of divorce is being proven wrong or misleading. The stepfamilies are adjusting the way a "normal" family does.

152. Robinson, Bryan E. "The Contemporary American Stepfather." *Family Relations* 33 (3: 1984): 381-88.

    The author focuses on data pertaining to stepfathers in previous stepfamily research and draws attention to the inconsistencies in the literature due to methological shortcomings.

153. Robinson, M. "Stepfamilies: A Reconstituted Family System." *Journal of Family Therapy* (2: 1980): 45-69.

154. Rosenbaum, Jean, M.D., and Veryl Rosenbaum. "Preparing Yourself to be Mother to His Children." *Woman* (August 1984): 42-43.

    This article focuses on the stepmother-stepchildren relationship, discussing feelings of rejection, comparisons between the real mother and the stepmother, and sexual attraction between the stepmother and a stepchild.

155. Rovner, Harriet. "Love Often Comes Before Trust
      in a Second Marriage." *Woman* (Auguat 1984): 43.

      This article briefly discusses, in a very light
      and humorous manner, legal realities, such as
      prenuptial agreements, which may need to be
      addressed before remarriage.

156. Rowlands, Peter. *Love Me, Love My Kids: A Guide
      for the New Partner.* New York: Continuum, 1983.

157. Rubenstein, Carin. "An Evolutionary Basis for
      Stepparents' Neglect?" *Psychology Today* 14
      (December 1980): 31, 100.

      Examines discriminatory parenting. Animals
      prefer their own and will reject offspring
      that are not their own. Stepparents are not
      given a chance to develop a close psychological
      attachment to their stepchildren. This may lead
      to child abuse and neglect. In 1976 there were
      87,789 validated cases of abused and neglected
      children in the United States. Stepchildren
      were two in seven times as likely to be abused
      as children living with their biological parents.

158. ————. "Forgiving the Linked Family."
      Psychology Today (April 1983): 59.

      The author discusses research being conducted
      by Doris Jacobson at UCLA on "linked family
      systems," two families who "share" a child. The
      study focuses on the relations between two
      separate households formed after a divorce and
      on how living with two families affects the
      children. The largest proportion of mothers
      and fathers said that visiting the other house-
      hold caused the most conflict and the greatest
      concern associated with this was the fear that
      the child would be ill-treated.

159. Sadler, Judith DeBoard. "Stepfamilies: An
      Annotated Bibliography." *Family Relations*
      32 (1: January 1983): 149-52.

This annotated bibliography contains twenty-one general works and three juvenile books and lists professional works, sociological studies, scholarly research, handbooks and guidebooks. Various aspects of step relationships are included, such as visitation arrangements, parenting agreements, shared custody, adoption by stepparents, weekend stepparents, stepsibling relationships, and guidelines for communicating. Also included is a listing of ten selected periodical articles.

160. Sager, Clifford J., Elizabeth Walker, Hollis Steer Brown, Helen M. Crohn, and Evelyn Rodstein. "Improving Functioning of the Remarried Family System." *Journal of Marital Family Therapy* 7 (1: January 1981): 3-13.

A report of issues in understanding and treating the remarried (rem) family. The need to include former spouses and to consider the metafamily system is discussed, along with treatment goals and various treatment modalities.

161. ―――. *Treating the Remarried Family.* New York: Brunner/Mazel, 1983.

Based on four and a half years of work with stepfamilies at the Remarried Consultation Service in New York City, this excellent book is a basic text for family therapists. The book is divided into four sections: Structure and Theory; Therapist and Treatment Strategies; Special Issues of Remarriage; and Preventative Measures.

162. ―――. "Remarriage Revisited." *Family and Child Mental Health Journal* 6 (1: 1980): 19-33.

This article surveys, updates and analyzes the literature written by professionals on remarriage, views the remarried family as a system, and outlines four areas of study that have been slighted. The four areas described are: (1) a failure to develop theoretical constructs; (2) lack of

treatment approaches; (3) lack of attention to
therapists and their emotional reactions; and
(4) lack of recognition of positive effects of
remarriage. The authors also suggest that successful remarried families have also been neglected
in the literature.

163. Santrock, John W., Cheryl L. Earshak, and Larry
        Meadows. "Children's and Parents' Observed
        Social Behavior in Stepfather Families."
        Child Development 53 (1982): 472-80.

        In this article, the authors set out to obtain
        more information about children and parents in
        stepfather families and specifically on their
        social behavior. The most consistent findings
        suggested that boys in stepfather families showed
        more competent social behavior than boys in intact
        families. Girls, by contrast, were found to be
        more anxious. Several factors implicated in
        children's social behavior are also discussed.

164. Schlesinger, Benjamin. *Remarriage: A Review
        and Annotated Bibliography*. Chicago: Council
        of Planning Librarians, 1983.

        This fully annotated bibliography covers
        remarriage related topics, such as adjustment,
        children, counseling, divorce, education,
        homosexuality, mate selection, myths, older
        persons, religion, single persons, stepfamilies,
        therapy and widowed individuals.

        Thirty-one journals were searched from 1961 to
        1982 (almost 75 percent of the articles appeared
        post-1976); the books found cover the period from
        1953 to 1982 (almost 62 percent have appeared
        since 1976.)

165. ————. "Remarriage in America and Canada: An
        Overview of the Literature, 1943-1980."
        Conciliation Courts Review 19 (1981): 21-36.

166. ————. *Remarriage in Canada: An Overview.*
      Toronto: University of Toronto, June 1983.

      This monograph discusses remarriage trends
      and research in Canada.

167. Schuchts, B.A., and B.K. Colvin. "Stepfamily
      Formation and Adaptation: A Theoretical
      Synthesis." Paper presented at the annual
      meeting of the National Council on Family
      Relations, Milwaukee, Wis., October 1981.

168. Schulman, Gerda L. "Divorce, Single Parenthood
      and Stepfamilies: Structural Implications of
      These Transactions." *International Journal
      of Family Therapy* 3 (2: Summer 1981): 87-112.

      This article deals primarily with changes that
      take place in the family structure during divorce.
      It also approaches the ideas of single parenthood
      and the reconstituted family. These reconstituted
      families have special challenges to face in order
      to function successfully. These challenges are
      discussed in light of various case studies. One
      important support system when a parent leaves or
      a stepparent is added to the home is family
      therapy. This article stresses the importance
      of working with both the person leaving and the
      person coming into the home. Effort must be put
      forth in order to build and maintain effective
      relationships.

169. Scott, Donald M. "Stepfamilies: A Historical
      Perspective." Conference proceedings at North
      Carolina State University, Raleigh, N.C., 1980.

170. Sell, R. "The Challenge of Stepparenting: A
      Bibliography." Paper presented at the annual
      meeting of the National Council on Family
      Relations, Portland, Ore., 1980.

171. Sheehy, P.T. "Family Enrichment for Stepfamilies:
      Empirical Study." Ph.D. dissertation. Purdue
      University, 1981.

172. Shipman, Gordon. "Reconstituted Families."
      Handbook for Family Analysis. Toronto:
      Lexington Books, D.C. Heath and Co., 1982,
      pp. 338-42.

      Myths and realities of reconstituted families
      are discussed. Suggestions to help overcome the
      difficulties that might be encountered are given.

173. Silber, Mark R. "Providing for Children When a
      Father Remarries." *Consumers Research*
      (December 1982): 41.

      The author, an attorney and consumer advocate,
      advises the first wife what to do in order to
      best provide for her own children and grandchild-
      ren in the event of her premature demise and of
      her husband's remarrying to avoid his using the
      assets from the first marriage to support a
      second wife and, if applicable, her children and
      neglecting his first children. Silber suggests
      that women in this situation get annual renew-
      able term insurance and, in this way, provide
      for her children and husband.

174. Silver, Gerald A., and Myrna Silver. *Weekend
      Fathers*. Los Angeles: Stratford Press, 1981.

      This book addresses a father's right in
      divorce cases. Problems of remarriage, second
      families and children's feelings are also
      discussed.

175. Sirulnik, Carole Ann. "The Primacy of the
      Couple and Stepfamily Integration: A Case
      Study Approach." Ph.D. dissertation.
      California School of Professional Psychology,
      1980.

This paper examined how four remarried couples reorganized their stepfamilies into integrated units and stressed that stepfamilies need to be considered satisfactory and potentially growth-producing alternative family constellations. Implications for clinicians were also discussed.

176. Skeen, Patsy, Bryan E. Robinson, and Carol Flake-Hobson. "Blended Families: Overcoming the Cinderella Myth." *Young Children* 39 (January 1984): 64-74.

This article explores research on stepfamilies (stepfathers, stepmothers and stepchildren), demographic information, the complexities of blended families and research findings, and gives teachers specific guidelines in working in the classroom, with the parents and with counselors. Very informative.

177. Smart, Laura S., and Mollie S. Smart. *Families: Developing Relationships.* New York: Macmillan Publishing Co., 1980.

Discusses the problems of reconstituted families. Money, self-consciousness, the real parent, hidden expectations, rivalry and competition between children and stepparent and parent, and success in families.

178. Spanier, G.B., and F.F. Furstenberg, Jr. "Remarriage Following Divorce: A Longitudinal Analysis." *Journal of Marriage and the Family* 44 (1982): 709-20.

179. Spanier, G.B., and P.C. Glick. "Marital Instability in the U.S.: Some Correlates and Recent Changes." *Family Relations* 30 (1981): 329-38.

180. ———. "Paths to Remarriage." *Journal of Divorce* 3 (3: 1980): 382-98.

181.   Spann, Owen, and Nancy Spann. *Your Child? I
       Thought It Was My Child.* New York: Pocket Books,
       1980.

       This book deals with all aspects of step-
       relations and is written in a dialogue fashion.
       Discipline, resentments, legal problems,
       adoption and holiday problems are among the
       topics covered.

182.   Steer, Mariann Hybels. "Projective Identification
       in Stepmother-Adolescent Stepdaughter Relation-
       ships." Ph.D. dissertation. California School
       of Professional Psychology, 1981.

       The purpose of this study was to identify
       variables contributing to the development of
       conflicted stepmother-adolescent stepdaughter
       relationships. Clinical applications were also
       discussed.

183.   Stenson, Janet Sigbert. *Now I Have a Stepparent
       and It's Kind of Confusing.* New York: Avon
       Books, 1980.

       This book focuses on the confusion children
       may feel when a parent remarries and the threat
       to their sense of security that remarriage poses.
       Can be read to or with a child and is helpfully
       illustrated.

184.   "Stepfamilies: Dealing with Anger and Disappoint-
       ment." *U.S. News and World Report* (January
       17, 1983): 67-68.

       This article is an interview with the author
       Elizabeth Einstein. It covers topics such as
       problems that crop up in stepfamilies, differ-
       ences in stepfamilies formed following a death
       rather than a divorce, how biological parents
       contribute to stepfamily problems, discipline
       issues, legal and financial responsibilities

of a stepparent, children's thoughts about
parents remarrying, support systems for stepfamilies, and benefits for stepfamilies.

185. "Stepparenting Problems: The Best Ways to Solve
    Them." *Good Housekeeping* (January 1984): 192.

    This easily readable article points out the
    most common problems occurring in stepfamilies,
    i.e., replacing a lost parent, adoption and
    inheritance rights, grandparents' rights, dif-
    ferent lifestyles, the stepparent and the
    school and health care coverage, and has advice
    from experts on how they can best be worked out.

186. Strother, J.F. "Adolescent Stress as it Relates
    to Stepfamily Living." Ed.D. dissertation.
    West Virginia University, 1981.

187. Stuart, Irving R., and Edwin Abt Lawrence.
    *Children of Separation and Divorce: Management
    and Treatment.* New York: Van Nostrand Reinhold
    Company, 1981.

    Strategies are given for working with the
    extended family in developing appreciation and
    respect of differences in people and in ways of
    living. Some areas covered are myths, absent
    parent and isolation of stepparent. Chapters
    13 and 14 are particularly informative.

188. Takai, Ricky Teruo. "Marital Separation in First
    Marriages and Remarriages in Women: An
    Examination of Divergent Patterns." Ph.D.
    dissertation. Johns Hopkins University, 1981.

    This paper examined several hypotheses ex-
    plaining why the rate of marital separation for
    remarried white women is higher than once-wed
    women, whereas the marital separation rate for
    black remarried women is lower or not signifi-
    cantly different than first married women.

189. "The Truth About Stepfamilies and How They Can
      Have a Perfectly Happy Household." *The Star*
      (April 17, 1984): 30.

      This article gives a list of the most destruc-
      tive myths about stepfamilies and suggests the
      facts that may lie behind them, as expressed by
      Richard and Patricia Bennett, co-founders of
      Listening, Inc., which provides counseling
      workshops and newsletters to stepfamilies.

190. Thies, Jill Mattews. "Beyond Divorce: The
      Impact of Remarriage on Children." *Journal of
      Clinical Child Psychology* 6 (2: Summer 1977):
      59-61.

      Remarriage is looked upon in this article as
      being as potentially traumatic to the child as
      divorce. Remarriage does not remove the pain
      inflicted by divorce, but rather gives rise to
      new and different complications. A child must
      deal with total structural changes in the family
      unit. This often occurs before a child has
      reconciled himself to the idea of having lost
      a parent through divorce. Many times that sense
      of loss may be accentuated by the the presence
      of a stepparent. A conflict arises within the
      child concerning where true loyalty should lie.
      It is pointed out that necessary changes must be
      made by individuals and institutions in order for
      children in this situation to emerge emotionally
      and psychologically intact.

191. Touliatos, John, and Byron W. Lindholm. "Teachers'
      Perceptions of Behavior Problems in Children
      from Intact, Single-Parent and Stepparent
      Families." *Psychology in the Schools* 17
      (2: April 1980): 264-69.

      A study of 3,644 white children in kindergarten-
      eighth grade in a suburban school district of
      Houston, Texas. 2,991 lived with both parents,
      312 mothers only, 43 with fathers only, 264

with mother and stepfather and 34 with father and stepmother. Teachers gave background information and checked a Behavior Problem Checklist. Children living with fathers only exhibited more socialized delinquency, children living with mothers and stepfathers showed more conduct problems and socialized delinquency and those living with father and stepmothers showed more conduct problems.

192. Tropf, W. "An Examination of Natural Father-Stepfather Responsibility for Parenting." Paper presented at the 44th annual meeting of the Florida Academy of Sciences, Tampa, Fla., 1980.

193. Trost, Jan E. "Remarriage in Sweden." *Family Relations* 33 (3: 1984): 475-81.

Reviews the rate of remarriage in couples divorced in 1971 and 1978. Also examines factors influencing remarriage and effects of remarriage on relations between former spouses.

194. Visher, Emily B., and John S. Visher. "Common Problems of Stepparents and Their Spouses." *American Journal of Orthopsychiatry* 48 (2: 1978): 252-62.

Four common stepfamily myths are discussed: (1) that a stepfamily is similar to an intact or nuclear family; (2) that death rather than divorce makes stepparenting less complicated; (3) that stepparenting is easier when the stepchildren visit rather than live with the stepparent; (4) and that love happens instantly. The common problems that are addressed are: (1) fighting the wicked stepmother myth; (2) dealing with guilt and sexuality; and (3) handling conflicts over discipline, divided loyalty, surnames and money.

195. ———. *Stepfamilies: A Guide to Working With Stepparents and Stepchildren.* New York: Brunner/ Mazel, 1979.

Drawing upon their personal and professional experiences, the authors have written a book which will be useful for both practicing therapists and those in training. After establishing the cultural context in which stepfamilies live today, the Vishers emphasize the structural characteristics which set stepfamilies apart from other family types. To provide realistic balance, the similarity of emotions experienced by persons seeking treatment, regardless of the family type, is acknowledged. Further, the research on stepfamily relationships (still rather limited) is reviewed.

The main part of the book contains a series of chapters focusing alternately on the interactional patterns of women, men, couples and children in stepfamilies. Each of these chapters is followed by a chapter providing suggestions for working with that particular subgroup.

The information presented certainly provides therapists with a basis for developing their own approach to working with this unique structural entity--the stepfamily.

196.   ———. "Stepfamilies in the 1980's." *Therapy with Remarriage Families*. Edited by James C. Hansen. Rockville, Md.: Aspen System Corp., (1982): 107-19.

Remarriage and recommitment is one phase of a process that starts after a divorce or the death of a parent, then moves through the single-parent household phase, and finally reaches the remarriage stage. What happens during each phase can be very important to the success of each succeeding phase.

Stepfamilies and professionals who work with them need to know that their family complexity can bring richness and diversity to their members.

Building new relationships makes stepfamily members sensitive to the importance of communication and emotional touching. Stepfamily members can experience the deep satisfaction and bonding that result from working together to meet difficult challenges.

197. ————. *Stepfamilies: Myths and Realities*. Secaucus, N.J.: Citadel Press, 1980.

This book was originally published as *Stepfamilies: A Guide to Working with Stepparents and Stepchildren*. This is a paperback version of Visher's book on stepfamilies. It is broad in scope and useful to those who want more information on the subject of stepfamilies.

198. Wald, Esther. *The Remarried Family: Challenge and Promise*. New York: Family Service Association of America, 1981.

This book addresses the need for new knowledge to help professionals who work with remarried families understand the realities unique to them. Based on clinical and research experience, it explores strengths, transitional processes and problems.

199. Walker, Glynnis. *Second Wife, Second Best?* New York: Doubleday, 1984.

Walker, a stepmother and founder of the Second Wives Association of North America, bases the material in her book on her own personal experiences and 1000 interviews. This book is a pragmatic look at marriage the second time around and addresses issues as diverse as stereotypes and sex.

200. Wallerstein, Judith S., and Joan B. Kelly. "Effects of Divorce on the Visiting Father-Child Relationship." *American Journal of Psychiatry* 137 (December 1980): 1534-39.

Discusses results of the authors' five year
Marin County, California, study of divorce on
children ages three to eighteen. Focus is on
the father-child relationships in a visiting
situation. Implications for stepfamilies.

201.   ————. *Surviving the Break-Up: How Children
and Parents Cope with Divorce*. New York: Basic
Books, 1980.

Based on research done to show the immediate
and long-range effects of divorce on childhood.
The authors concentrate on children, ages
three to eighteen, and their feelings after the
divorce.

Children's feelings during the separation make
up the first section of the book. The authors
then address the parent-child relationship after
separation. A five year follow-up period is
dealt with in the last section. A bibliography
is provided.

202.   Walter, J., and L.H. Walter. "Parent-Child
Relationships: A Review, 1970-1979." *Journal
of Marriage and the Family* 42 (1980): 807-22.

203.   Ware, Ciji. *Sharing Parenthood After Divorce:
An Enlightened Custody Guide for Mothers,
Fathers, and Kids*. New York: Viking Press,
1982.

Ware, a strong supporter of joint custody, has
written a step-by-step guide from the warning
signals of possible divorce to the day-to-day
details of managing child care in two separate
households. It has information on communicating
with a former spouse, a lawyer, or a judge, plus
advice that takes into consideration the ages
of the children and the emotional and financial
states of the parents. It includes checklists,
possible scenarios and samples of shared custody
agreements that are now working for families all
over the country.

204. Warnat, Winifred I. *Guide to Parent Involvement:*
      Parents as Adult Learners. Annotated Bibliog-
      raphy on the Family. Washington, D.C.: American
      University, Adult Learning Potential Institute,
      1980. (ERIC Document Reproduction Service No.
      ED 198-373.)

      This document is the last in a series of four
      reports developed to provide an overview of parent
      involvement with regard to the family, parenting
      needs and existing resources, along with parent
      education approaches and practices. This partic-
      ular document is an annotated bibliography that
      presents short descriptions of publications that
      relate to the family. Special consideration is
      given to parent education.

205. Weingarten, H. "Remarriage and Well-Being:
      National Survey Evidence of Social and
      Psychological Effects." *Journal of Family*
      Issues 1 (4: 1980): 533-59.

206. Westoff, Leslie Aldridge. "Stepchildren: Yours
      and His." *Harper's Bazaar* (January 1981):
      89, 136-37.

      Explores all of the issues related to children
      in a stepfamily situation, pays particular
      attention to the issues of gaining a parent and
      privacy, and offers a few words of encouragement.

207. Wheeler, Michael. *Divided Children: A Legal*
      Guide for Divorcing Parents. New York:
      Norton, 1980.

      Written as a guide for parents dealing with
      custody laws and other legal problems.

      It addresses such issues as who wins custody,
      how much child support is right for a particular
      family, how much a lawyer should be paid, how to
      change an unsuccessful custody agreement and
      other divorce issues. The book will help
      divorcing people to understand the custody
      system in our country.

208. Whiteside, M.F. "Remarriage: A Family Developmental Process." *Journal of Marital and Family Therapy* (April 1982).

209. Wilson, Kenneth L. "Stepfathers and Stepchildren." *Journal of Marriage and the Family* 12 (August 1979): 16-20.

      An exploratory analysis of two national surveys. It discusses the relationship of stepfathers and their stepchildren--the problems and successes.

210. Wines, Leslie. "A New Kind of Stepmother." *Glamour* 8 (August 1983): 140-46.

      Family therapists are seeing more women in their twenties and thirties whose fathers have remarried women close to their daughter's age. The great rise in divorce among middle-aged people and more liberal ideas about whom it is appropriate to date have made this type of remarriage an option for more people. For many women, the biggest problem of a young stepmother is simply feeling awkward in different situations. Some say they feel abandoned and betrayed if their fathers remarry. The most severe problems occur when daughters feel pushed out of their father's nests before they're ready to leave. A closeness is needed, one that is not based on a childhood image or idolization, but one on a realistic expectation of each other.

211. Woodruff, C. Roy. "Counseling for Remarrieds." *Home Life* 38 (3: December 1983): 10-11.

      The author, a marriage counselor, raises some probing questions and addresses some Christian issues in remarriage. He discusses the dynamics of mate selection, potentially painful realities in remarriages and hopeful possibilities.

212. Wooley, Persia. *The Custody Handbook*. New York: Simon and Schuster, 1980.

An excellent handbook on custody which presents a strong argument for co-parenting and deals with legal issues in divorce.

213. Yoder, J.D., and R.C. Nichols. "A Life Perspective Comparison of Married and Divorced Persons." *Journal of Marriage and the Family* (42: 1980): 413-19.

PARENTS' BIBLIOGRAPHY

There are very few bibliographies available for the
lay public, particularly parents. This section includes
books generally available in public libraries and
articles found in magazines and newspapers in the past
few years. This list for parents should also be helpful
for professionals who are novices in the field of stepfamilies and want an introduction to the issues involved.

214. Albert, Linda. *Linda Albert's Advice for Coping
     With Kids*. New York: E.P. Dutton, Inc., 1982.

     A guidebook written to help parents in raising
     children. A chapter entitled "Dealing with
     Divorce and Remarriage" covers expectations,
     visiting routines, enforcing rules, staying out
     of stepchildren's squabbles and dealing with
     picking on younger stepbrothers and sisters.

     It is written in a question-answer format.
     There is a chapter specifically dealing with
     stepparenting with a list of guidelines for a
     stepparent to use in dealing with his/her new
     family.

215. Anderson, Gail S., and Hal W. Anderson. *Mom and
     Dad Are Divorced, But I'm Not*. Chicago:
     Nelson-Hall, 1981.

     This book focuses on children's responses and,
     while paying full attention to the problems that

the marriage partner faces as an individual, also
succeeds in making the reader see the child's
point of view.

Chapter 12 specifically addresses stepparenting.
There is a list for positive stepparenting and
things for stepparents to remember. The issues
of part-time stepparents as well as summertime
stepparents is also addressed, along with money
matters, mothers and stepmothers.

216. Atwell, Anthony E., Ursula S. Moore, and Carla
      S. Nowell. "The Role of Stepparents in Child
      Custody Disputes." *Bulletin of the AAPL* 10
      (3: 1982): 211-17.

The authors define a stepfamily as one in which
at least one of the adults is a stepparent. A
stepparent's approach is related to his values and
goals. A positive influence is more often presented by a stepparent who has not had children
prior to this marriage. Children benefit also
when there is compatability between biological
parents and stepparents in child-rearing practices
and general lifestyle issues. The biological
parents and stepparents share the responsibility
for defining their new roles. According to the
authors, children who feel they are caught in a
bind between the two forces suffer from symptoms
of anxiety, depression, withdrawal and acting out.

217. Berger, Stuart, M.D. *Divorce Without Victims*.
      Boston: Houghton Mifflin Company, 1983.

Provides insights and tools parents need to
help their children deal with the difficult
emotional problems caused by divorce. Explained
are the dangers inherent in leaning on the
opposite-sex child--the mother who depends on her
son as "man of family" or father who depends on his
daughter to "manage" the household. It also
describes the difference between grief and depression, the signals indicating that outside help is
needed and where to get it.

Attention is focused on remarriage and the complex relationships of the stepfamily and emotional growth in stepfamilies in the first year.

218. Berman, Claire. *Making It as a Stepparent, New Roles/New Rules*. New York: Doubleday & Co., 1980.

All angles of the stepfamily situation: the role that money plays in a family formed by remarriage; the decisions involved in setting up a new household or moving into an established one; the confusion of merging two or more different life styles, sets of rules, methods of discipline, different names; the shock experienced by the childless individual who becomes an "instant parent" by marrying someone with children; the alienation of a child who loses a natural parent and then gains a new guardian, perhaps new brothers and sisters, as well; the guilt of a parent who lives with the children of his current spouse while his own offspring are in the custody of another; the tension of the non-custodial parent and her visiting children; the pros and cons of having a common child. The book offers help in overcoming the fears, doubts and disillusionments that can affect the stepparenting situation.

219. ———. "Stepfamilies--A Growing Reality." *Public Affairs Pamphlet* 609 (1982). Illustrated by Anna Marie Magagna.

This pamphlet deals with all aspects of the stepfamily. Included are: myths that intrude on the stepfamily, the instant parent, terminology, age of the children as a factor, situations where the first parent has died, where to set up home, discipline, looking at the financial picture, visitation, considerations of a sexual nature, holidays and other special occasions, adopting a stepchild and ways to acquire help.

220. ————. "The Instant Parent." *Redbook Magazine*
      (1981): 118-72.

      The most difficult adjustment in a marriage
      is for the man or woman who doesn't have children
      and marries someone who does. At that moment
      that person becomes an instant parent. There
      may be a power struggle over who has authority
      over whom. Couples must deal with whose money
      goes for what. The author of this article
      stresses the idea of compromise. Research says
      that it takes from three to five years for most
      people to adjust to new personalities and routines
      and to think of themselves as "a family."

221. Brooks, J.B. *The Process of Parenting*. Palo
      Alto: Mayfield, 1981.

      The book was written for couples preparing
      for parenthood and as a help to improve the
      effectiveness of parents. Extensive guidelines
      and background information are supplied so the
      reader can accomplish the basic tasks of parenting.

      In later chapters, discussions are presented
      about women's views on entering the work force
      and the possible effects of mother's employment
      on children. Next, single parents are discussed
      by focusing on how to cope with the disruptions
      of the family unit. Dealing with the loss and
      establishment of a new life pattern is addressed,
      including guidelines for support. Included in
      this section is a table of stressfulness in life
      events.

      The last chapter in the book lists resources
      parents can draw on when their children face
      severe problems. The text is written in a
      professional manner but also readable for
      any interested or concerned parent.

222. Bustanoby, Andre. *The Readymade Family: How to be a Stepparent and Survive*. Grand Rapids: Zondervan Publishing House, 1982.

This book seeks to adapt to stepfamilies as many of the biblical and psychological principles of natural parenthood as possible. The author helps to sort out the complex emotions that the various members bring into the new household and to deal constructively with the conflicting forces that cross the threshold of the home.

223. Cate, Rodney M. "Reconstructed Families." *Christian Single* 5 (10: January 1984): 39.

This article says stepparents face some unique problems they may not have encountered in their first marriages. Using research from the National Institute of Mental Health, the author suggests ways individuals or couples can go about preventing problems that could arise in reconstructed families and offers some guidelines for dealing with child rearing.

224. Chapman, Gracie. "A Very Special Wedding." *Good Housekeeping* 199 (70: August 1984): 70-72.

The article focuses on the experiences of a woman who married a widower and who had to assume responsibility for planning a wedding for her stepdaughter. She didn't lose a daughter-- she gained one.

225. ———. "His, Mine...Ours." *Good Housekeeping* 195 (November 1982): 104-9.

Describes the personal account of the blending of two families. The adults involved were a divorcee and widower, six children ranging in age from 9 to 19, and the widower's mother-in-law. The author shares the story of their introduction, courtship, wedding, honeymoon and two years of working out a happy family relationship. She dealt with the "wicked stepmother" myth as well

as details like grocery shopping for a family of
nine. The underlying advice is not to dwell on
the problems, but emphasize the family.

226.   Collins, Glenn. "Stepfamilies Share Their Joys
         and Woes." *New York Times* (October 24, 1983).

This article presents the census figure of
the growing number of stepfamilies, talks about
the conference of the Stepfamily Association of
America held in the Blue Ridge Mountains, October
22-23, 1983 and the issues raised there, mentions
the composition of several stepfamilies and
explains more about the Stepfamily Association
of America.

227.   Craven, Linda. *Stepfamilies: New Patterns of
         Harmony*. New York: Simon and Schuster, 1982.

Each chapter in this book tells a story of a
young person who had to adjust to the problems
of stepfamilies. These stories are actual case-
histories and deal with real problems and real
solutions. The stepparent's side of the story
is also given.

This book would be good for parents because
they could view the situation from the eyes of
their children as well as from their own point
of view. Teenagers could benefit from this book
by seeing that their own situations are not
unique.

228.   Crook, Roger H. "New Roles in Remarriage."
         Home Life 38 (January 1984): 22-23.

Presented in this article are some problems
facing remarrieds along with some possible
solutions to the problems. The problems that
are discussed are those of adjusting to a second
spouse, adjusting to stepchildren, adjusting to
a former spouse and dealing effectively with
the past.

229. Drescher, Joan E. *Your Family, My Family*. New York: Walker, 1980.

Briefly describes several kinds of families and cites some of the strengths of family life.

230. Eddy, Carol. "That First Christmas Together." *Ladies' Home Journal* (December 1981): 19-20.

The author tells in a light-hearted, but honest way, how her stepfamily, consisting of his six children and her four children, developed from territorial warring tribes, each with its own rules and traditions, into a cohesive, loving famiy. The article describes step-by-step the new family's first Christmas Eve and Christmas together.

231. Edelman, Alice, and Roz Stuzin. *How to Survive a Second Marriage (Or Save a First One)*. Secaucus, N.J.: Lyle Stuart Inc., 1980.

The reality of what confronts those contemplating remarriage is presented. Personal stories from some who have learned to cope in a second marriage are given to help and give confidence to the remarried family.

232. Einstein, E. "Five Myths about Stepfamilies." *Parents* (November 1983): 90-91.

The author deals with myths about stepfamilies from the perspective of a stepparent. The myths presented are: (1) making a stepfamily is as simple as saying "I do"; (2) stepfamilies work like nuclear families; (3) instant love occurs among stepfamily members; (4) part-time stepfamily living is easier than fulltime; (5) stepfamilies form easier from death than divorce.

233. ————. "Stepfamilies--Dealing with Anger and Disappointment." *U.S. News and World Report* (January 17, 1983): 67, 68.

In question and answer format, the author, a
stepparent, shares insightfully some common
knowledge. This is a good short article packed
with a variety of information about remarriage
and stepchildren's adjustments.

234.   Einstein, Elizabeth, and Linda Albert. *The
       Stepfamily Living Series*. Tampa, Fla.: South-
       print Corp., 1983.

These booklets explore different aspects of
stepfamily life. Full of hints and concrete
suggestions that every parent and stepparent
can apply. Includes: preparing for remarriage;
pitfalls and possibilites; dealing with discipline
and encouragement and enrichment.

235.   Englund, C.L. "Parenting and Parentage: Distinct
       Aspects of Children's Importance." *Family
       Relations: Journal of Applied Family and
       Child Studies* 32 (1: January 1983): 21-28.

Discusses information from interviews showing
that children add a special dimension to the
lives of their parents and grandparents. There
are implications for prospective parents and
grandparents, adoptive parents and the childless.

236.   Evans, Patsy. "When a Parent Remarries." *Home
       Life* 38 (6: March 1984): 37-39.

This article tells how a young married woman
learned to cope with her seventy-four year old
father's remarriage. Her resentment stemmed
from this woman, a stranger, using her mother's
dishes, cookware and silver and sleeping in her
mother's bed. The author had not completely
resolved her conflict but described her change
in attitude and acceptance of the situation.

237. Felker, Evelyn H. *Raising Other People's Kids:
Successful Child Rearing in the Restructured
Family*. Grand Rapids, Mich.: Erdmans, 1981.

Guide to methods of dealing with encounters
that will arise in the stepfamily situation.

238. Francke, Linda Bird. *Growing Up Divorced*.
New York: Linden Press, Simon and Schuster, 1983.

Helping your child through the stages of
growing up divorced is the main focus of this
book. It begins with infants and continues
through the teenage years. It explains why one
child's guilt is another child's anger.

Chapters nine and ten focus on steplives. It
covers pitfalls, failed expectations and
the schools. The book is very informative and
easy to read.

The book gives concrete suggestions for
parents to help their children adjust to divorce
and steplives.

239. Francke, Linda Bird, and Michael Reese. "After
Remarriage." *Newsweek* (February 11, 1980): 66.

The divorce rate is higher in second marriages
mainly because of the strain of working out all
the blended family crises. The children feel
defeated in not preventing the divorce, and
feel defeated again for not preventing the
remarriage. Confusion occurs for them as they
juggle the different rules and values and perhaps
gain instant sets of stepsisters and stepbrothers.

240. Gilbert, Sara D. *Trouble at Home*. New York:
Lothrop, Lee and Shepard, 1981.

Examines positive responses to common problems
such as death, divorce, or troublesome siblings
that may disrupt family life.

241. Glass, Stuart M. *A Divorce Dictionary: A*
      Book for You and Your Children. Boston:
      Little, Brown, 1980. Illustrated by Bari
      Weissman.

      This dictionary defines terms of divorce, such
      as: custody, visitation, stepfamily and so on,
      by explaining what each one means and through
      stories and case histories, how it applies in
      actual instances.

      This book can help parents and children under-
      stand how laws affect and influence them now and
      in the future, in the case of divorce or in the
      event of a family restructure.

242. Grossman, Mary Ann. "The Second Wives: Haunted
      by Ghosts Past." *The Atlanta Constitution*
      (June 28, 1984): 1.

      Interview of Glynnis Walker, writer of *Second*
      Wife, Second Best? She shares a personal account
      of her stepfamily situation. A successful,
      well-educated columnist, Ms. Walker thought she
      could handle anything. She found out differently
      after marrying a man with three grown children.
      Several myths about stepfamilies are examined.

243. Hamilton, Elsie. "Being a Stepfamily Magnifies
      Everyday Problems." *The Gastonia Gazette*
      197 (September 23, 1983): 48.

      Focuses on Dana and Bob Crunketon who are old
      hands at being stepparents. They joined the
      Stepfamilies of America chapter in Gastonia,
      North Carolina, to help others who are going
      through situations they had experienced. Dana
      and Bob usually tell stepparents to handle a
      problem the same way they would with their own
      children. Just use common sense. She recommends
      never putting down the real parent of stepchildren.
      That is a sure way of driving the child back to
      the natural parent. Mrs. Crunketon credits her

husband with the missing link in her family.
She stresses the importance of parents sharing
the same values.

244. Hedger, Christine L. "Mending a Broken Family."
Home Life 38 (5: February 1984): 18-21.

This article tells the story of two small girls
who were physically and sexually abused by their
stepfather. It relates brief family history
and explains how they were reunited.

245. "How to Be a Stepparent." *Business Week* (March
28, 1983): 148-49.

This article discusses the rising number of
stepfamilies and the problems which these families
face. Several stepparents tell about situations
which they encountered as a stepparent. Included
is a short list of books and organizations for
stepfamilies.

246. "How to Handle a Wedding the Second Time Around--
With Children." *Glamour* 4 (April 1981): 245.

Remarrying when you and/or your husband-to-be
have children means the start of a new life for
everyone. Couples who want their wedding day to
mark the beginning of a new family as well as a
new marriage, include the children. The article
provides helpful tips for breaking the news,
involving them in the plans, the ceremony and
the reception.

247. "I Couldn't Accept My Father's Remarriage."
Good Housekeeping 199 (August 1984): 36.

The article focuses on the resentment felt
by a woman when her father divorced her mother
and remarried a young wife. She has learned
to accept the fact that she must live with the
choice her father has made and has taken practical
steps to adapt to the changes in the family.

248.   Ivey, Dick.   "Parenting/Blended Families."
        Christian Single 3 (4: July 1981): 40-41.

        The author says blending families is like
        mixing water and oil.   He had hoped his new
        family would function like a natural family,
        but it didn't and still doesn't.   He suggests
        approaching a blended family as you would two
        porcupines making love--very carefully.   Parenting
        responsibilities are the biggest headaches.   He
        offers sixteen suggestions that help in coping
        with a blended family.

249.   Jacobson, Doris S.   "Stepfamilies." *Children
        Today* (January-February 1980): 5.

        This article emphasizes the identification
        and anticipation of difficulties in stepfamily
        life and how satisfaction can be gained from
        membership in this family arrangement.

250.   Jensen, Larry C., and Janet M. Jensen.   *Stepping
        into Stepparenting: A Practical Guide*.   Palo
        Alto: R & E Research Associates, Inc., 1981.

        Emphasizes the importance of developing
        realistic perceptions and goals for stepfamilies.
        After pointing out how to move in a positive
        direction, an easy-to-use system of family
        organization is presented.   This system is based
        on providing more positive outcomes and is
        followed by a chapter on how to enrich family
        life after increased love and trust has had time
        to develop.   The last section of the book contains
        solutions for the most stressful problems facing
        stepparents.

251.   Jolin, Peter.   *How to Succeed as a Stepparent*.
        New York: New American Library, 1981.

        This book shows how stepparents can prevent
        falling into frustrating, enraging, bitter con-
        flicts with stepchildren.   It offers concrete
        advice on bonding, understanding feelings,
        communicating and discipline.

252. Kalter, Suzy. *Instant Parent: A Guide for Stepparents, Part-Time Parents, and Grand-Parents.* New York: A & W Publishers, Inc., 1979.

Written by a stepparent, this book is a helpful guide for "instant" parents going through the steps of caring for someone else's children. There is advice for the first meeting, buying clothing, how to travel with children, medicine, discipline, titles and other child-related situations. The author has included many helpful lists: common childhood illnesses, what to keep in the medicine cabinet, how to deal with tears and bed-wetting and similar crises.

253. Lewis, Helen Coale. *All About Families the Second Time Around.* Atlanta, Ga.: Peachtree Publishers, 1980.

This book is a guide to the formation of new relationships and is written simply enough for children as well as parents to understand. It also includes worksheets to help children understand their new situation as a stepchild. It explains feelings of anger and sadness that children may have in their relationships with stepparents. The messages in this book are designed to help stepfamilies explore the many choices available to them in creating something new together, new traditions that recognize and respect differences between first and second time around families.

254. Lewis-Steere, Cynthia. *Stepping Lightly.* Minneapolis, Minn.: CompCare Publications, 1981.

In this A to Z guide, the author suggests that humor and a stepparent group may be the most important aids for successful stepparenting. Each letter of the alphabet has a stepfamily issue associated with it. The author also suggests that each parent should speak for himself and

express his own needs and feelings, rather than
play ventriloquist. The last half of the book
is a weekly guide, where family, couple, individual and stepparent group goals can be
recorded.

255. Lippi, Otty. *The Second Time Around*. New York:
     Dembner Books, 1981.

     This book is a narrative about Otty Lippi's
     real experiences in trying to adjust to widowhood.
     It covers all her attempts at starting again and
     the unwanted as well as wanted advice of family
     and friends. She goes through many experiences
     trying to adjust to her new way of living and
     trying to find someone who really cares. Through
     it all, she keeps her sense of humor.

256. List, Julie Autumn. *The Day the Loving Stopped*.
     New York: Seaview Books, 1980.

     This book is a first-person account of a
     daughter's view of her life with her parents,
     stepbrothers and sister during and following her
     parents' divorce. The author records her feelings
     and her search for the things she thought were
     missing in her life.

257. "Local Stepfamilies Join Together for Support."
     The Gastonia Gazette 197 (September 23, 1983):
     2B.

     A chapter of Stepfamilies Association of America
     was formed in Gastonia, North Carolina, by Rev.
     Fred Fales, an associate pastor of First Methodist
     Church. A support group was needed to help
     families learn what other families were doing and
     think about what they should do. People in the
     group learned how to communicate with each other.
     Speakers at the stepfamily meetings have included
     a child psychologist, who talked about children's
     feelings in relation to divorce and marriage,
     and a family counselor, who discussed family
     communication. The best thing the families have
     discovered is that they are not alone.

258. Louie, Elaine. "The Newest Extended Family."
     House and Garden (July 1981): 16-20.

     This article states: "A stepfamily is a
     college of people." It discusses flawed myths;
     roles of aunts, uncles, moms and dads; rules
     and discipline and how to share your children.

259. Lovett, Lois. "Stepmothering: Am I Ready For
     This?" *Ms.* 9 (November 1982): 114.

     A personal account. The article briefly
     discusses strategies for stepparenting, conflicts
     with stepchildren, conflicts with ex-spouses,
     misunderstandings between the husband and his
     new wife concerning the children and negative
     feelings which may arise because of the new
     stepmothering situation. The author does an
     excellent job describing her innermost feelings
     about her trying situation as an "instant" mother.

260. Meredith, K. "I Married My Husband's Kids."
     Parents 61 (11: 1983): 87-94.

     A personal account of a young woman dealing
     with the problems of dating and marrying a man who
     has children by a previous marriage. She learns
     to experience emotions never imagined before she
     became a stepmother. She learns to share her
     new husband's attention with his children and
     handle the loyalty felt towards the real mother.
     Anger, jealousy and guilt were emotions that had
     to be confronted in her attempts to be a good
     stepparent.

261. Miner, Robert. "Does the Second Wife Play
     Second Fiddle?" *Redbook* 162 (2: January 1984):
     62.

     The author points to the fact that the husband
     is the man in the middle, torn between two
     families, the wife is the one who must wait while
     he works things out. The dice are loaded against
     even the most determined stepmother.

262. Moser, Becky. "A Stepmother's True Confessions."
      The Gastonia Gazette 83 (April 21, 1983): 4B.

      Personal experiences of the author involving
      her stepson and herself. She and Steve liked
      each other and did things together but neither
      one loved the other. She began to resent having
      to do her "mothering" duties and getting little
      respect for it. She began to feel like a maid
      and resented that. It made her feel guilty. The
      stage was set for her to become the wicked old
      stepmother. Then she discovered that these feel-
      ings were typical. She and her family now cope
      with the idea they will never be a "real" family.
      It's still tough sometimes but they are working
      on becoming a family with its own identity.

263. Mulford, Phillippa Greene. "Stepparenting: How
      to Star in a Challenging Role." *Vogue* 171
      (9: September 1981): 258, 263.

      A young couple, both in their second marriage,
      is faced with problems raising two children. The
      woman became an instant mother with all her
      responsibilities being compounded because they fell
      on the weekends. After a time she found that being
      consistent with the children made the new family
      function in a happier atmosphere.

264. Neisser, Judith. "Are You Ready for Stepchil-
      dren?" *Harper's Bazaar* (3260: July 1983):
      57-58, 152.

      The article presents questions and answers
      on the subject of stepparenting. One point
      brought out in the article is the "pink cloud
      syndrome." This is the feeling that a woman
      views her prospective stepmother role over-
      optimistically. Wedding plans need to go slowly.
      Start out in a fresh environment. It is also
      important that both parents be supportive of one
      another. One stepmother summed it up, "Imagine
      the warm feeling you will get when you realize
      you're no longer thinking of them as stepchil-
      dren, they're your children."

265. Norman, Michael. "The New Extended Family: Divorce Reshapes the American Household." *New York Times Magazine* (November 23, 1980).

   Describes three families extended through divorce and remarriage.

266. Norment, Lynn. "Should You Marry Someone With Children." *Ebony* XXXVIII (1: November 1982): 101-4.

   This article discusses whether you should marry someone with children. You need to weigh the pros and cons. Most people prefer to marry people without children, but when in love, people tend to ignore the problems regarding children. It is important that couples have serious talks about the children before getting married. Ask yourself questions.

267. ————. "Stepchildren-Stepparent: Must There Always Be Conflict?" *Ebony* 83 (January 1981): 83-89.

   The author of this article discusses the challenge of being stepparents and maintains that conflicts do not always have to exist. She expresses her hope that with more education and better understanding, society will perhaps realize that the stepfamily not only shares many of the same problems as the natural family unit, but also much of its joy and love. She lists twelve interesting ways of how to be a good stepparent.

268. Parrish, Michael. "At Twenty-Six, How Could I Be a Father to a Ten-Year Old Girl." *Glamour* 9 (September 1983): 237, 238, 248.

   A stepfather's point of view about the problems he encountered as he became an instant father of a ten year old when he was only twenty-six years old himself. At the writing of this article, the

marriage had succeeded for ten years and seemed
to be stable. The author said the stability of
the marriage determined the success of the stepfamily.

269. Porterfield, Kay Marie. "Surviving and Thriving
      With Your Stepparent." *Seventeen* (October
      1981): 166-67, 178, 180.

      A daughter's viewpoint on stepparents as she
      later looks on a relationship that can be special.
      Ideas are given to help with tension between
      stepchild and stepparent. Several ways for
      easing the transition from a divorce to accepting
      a new family situation are given throughout the
      article. Stepparents usually want to build a
      good relationship as much as a stepchild.

270. Roberts, Francis. "Stepfamilies: Stresses and
      Surprises." *Parents* 3 (March 1981): 108.

      The Department of Health and Human Services
      estimates that there are between eight and ten
      million children living in stepfamilies and very
      likely many more who have stepparents with whom
      they don't live. These more complex family
      relationships create new pressures for children
      involved, such as blurred identity and differing
      values. But findings reflect a changing view
      of family arrangements in a society in which it
      is no longer unusual to have stepparents or to
      be a stepchild. Whether this is good news or bad
      news depends on your own values and circumstances
      but it does seem to call for a reexamination of
      some of our assumptions.

271. Rosenbaum, Jean, and Veryl Rosenbaum. *Living
      With Teenagers* New York: Stein and Day Publish-
      ers, 1980.

      Chapter IX explains how to be an effective
      stepparent. It deals with such topics as the
      need for approval or acceptance by the stepchild;

how to discipline the teenage stepchild effectively; how to cope with jealousy on both the
stepchild's and stepparent's part. It deals
with the sexual attraction an older stepchild
may have toward the stepparent. The chapter
discusses the importance of stepparents joining
an existing family instead of creating a new one.

272. Rowlands, Peter. "Love Him, Love His Kids."
     Cosmopolitan (July 1984): 98.

     Discusses ways to prepare for meeting your
     mate's children. It stresses the importance of
     making advance preparations. Your partner can
     set the stage with his child to make things go
     smoother. Nine practical suggestions are shared.

273. ———. *Saturday Parent--A Book for Separated
     Families*. New York: Continuum Publishing Corp.,
     1980.

     This book is written specifically for the parent
     who lives apart from his or her natural children.
     It gives individual cases of children and their
     divorced parents and the many problems encountered
     by them. Chapter Eight deals specifically with
     the issues of coping with your child's new step-
     parent. It approaches the loyalty conflict,
     lack of time available, resentment of being
     supplanted, problems with names, conflicts in
     customs and behavior, stepparent stories and
     stepsiblings.

274. Salk, L. *The Complete Dr. Salk*. New York: New
     American Library, 1983.

     It is the author's contention that "it is
     easier to prevent emotional ills in infancy and
     early childhood than to treat them later in life.
     That is the reason for this book." The book is
     arranged in A to Z encyclopedia format, with
     cross referencing. In the section on stepparents,
     the author emphasizes the need for patience and

understanding as a basis for the establishment
of a comfortable situation with a new family.
He encourages family counseling in situations
in which apparent incompatibilities continue.

275. Sands, Melissa. *The Second Wife's Survival
      Manual*. New York: Berkley Books, 1982.

      Part Three, "Stategies for Parenting,"
      includes a test for preconceived notions about
      being a stepparent.

276. Seixas, Suzanne. "When Three Plus Two Equal One."
      Money 12 (4: April 1983): 89-90.

      Discusses in much detail the lives of two
      divorced people and how they and their children
      become one blended family. It tells of the
      readjustments involved in a stepfamily situation.
      Deals primarily with the finances of this family.

277. Silverweig, Mary Zenorini. *The Other Mother*.
      New York: Harper and Row, 1982.

      The Other Mother is Ms. Silverzweig's true
      story of her life with her husband and her step-
      family--his three daughters. She describes the
      first seven years of their life together--its
      considerable joys and all the anger, resentment,
      guilt and conflict that accompany a marriage
      in which the freight of an earlier family is an
      unremitting presence.

278. "Stepparenting Problems: The Best Ways to Solve
      Them." *Good Housekeeping* 1 (January 1984): 192.

      Several common problems occurring in stepfamilies
      were listed along with advice on how to deal with
      them. A serious emotional problem faced is the
      loss of a parent. The stepparent must make it
      clear that he or she isn't trying to replace the
      natural parent. It is suggested couples decide
      how they want their household to run and once

decisions are agreed upon, support one another and present them to the children, allowing them some input. In the matter of discipline, leave the disciplining up to the natural parent initially. Courts are now addressing the grandparent's rights. Five states now have provisions that allow grandparents to see their grandchildren.

279. Stewart, Marjabelle Young. *The New Etiquette Guide to Getting Married Again*. New York: St. Martin's Press, 1980.

This book is a guide to an appropriate second wedding. It is filled with imaginative ideas for special wedding ceremonies, receptions, etc. It contains advice on coping with problems and emotions surrounding remarriages, such as becoming a stepparent, forming new relationships with in-laws, merging two households or beginning a new one, merging two careers, making decisions about financial arrangements and in some cases, drawing up a marriage contract.

280. Thayer, Nancy. *Stepping*. New York: Doubleday, 1980.

One of the first novels to concentrate on the stepmother-stepchild relationship, from early childhood into the twenties. There are insights into many areas that can cause problems and a view of the terrible hostility that can be aroused by a new baby. Stepmothers will readily identify with this book.

281. Troyer, Warner. *Divorced Kids*. New York: Harcourt Brace Jovanovich, 1980.

Children of divorce are interviewed. They speak out and give advice to mothers, fathers, lovers, stepparents, sisters, brothers and each other.

282. Turnbull, Sharon K., and James M. Turnbull. "To Dream the Impossible Dream: An Agenda for Discussion with the Stepparents." *Family Relations* 32 (April 1983): 227-30.

This article deals with the many dilemmas that
arise in stepparenting which many stepparents
find themselves ill-equipped to handle. Often
these problems are not discussed openly and
dealt with, which increases their effect on the
newly structured family. Ten major guidelines
are given to aid in the stepparenting process.
These guidelines include the ideas of neutral
territory, role identity, setting and enforcing
limits, providing outlets for feelings, culti-
vating love, division of responsibility and the
need for general patience.

283. Visher, Emily B., and John S. Visher. *How to
      Win as a Stepfamily*. New York: Red Dembner
      Enterprises Corp., 1982.

      The authors have written this book from a
      first-hand point of view, in that each had
      custody of four children from a previous marriage
      when they married. *How to Win as a Stepfamily*,
      offers advice on problems that are likely to
      arise in the course of remarrying and creating
      a stepfamily, on false expectations that can
      become stumbling blocks for stepparents and
      children and on ways to build new relationships
      and preserve old ones. According to the authors,
      stepfamilies can be good families in which to
      raise children and find personal satisfaction
      and growth.

284. Walker, Glynnis. "Is Second Wife, Second Best?"
      People Weekly, 22 (July 23, 1984): 75.

      The author explores the pitfalls of being spouse
      number two in this interview article.

285. Watrous, Peter. "Step-Etiquette." *Psychology
      Today* 18 (80: January 1984): 80.

      The author briefly points out that etiquette
      books offer little guidance for handling "steps"
      and "exes." Emily Post and Amy Vanderbilt provide

advice only about simple stepproblems. The
author suggests deciding on what to do for
yourself.

286. "When Your New Spouse's Children Give You a
      Hard Time." *Business Week* 47 (October 27, 1980):
      189-90.

      It is estimated that forty percent of second
      marriages end in divorce. Often each member of
      the new family enters into the arrangement with
      widely divergent goals and unrealistic expecta-
      tions. The article listed five guidelines to
      ease the strain that a new relationship may
      cause. A list of books was also provided to help.

287. Westoff, Leslie A. "Stepchildren: Yours and His."
      Harper's Bazaar (January 1981): 89.

      Explores a second marriage and how often it
      is more than a blending of two lives--it may be a
      merger of many. Trying to create harmony out of
      disparity is one of the most difficult challenges
      of marrying into a prefabricated family.

CHILDREN'S AND YOUNG ADULTS BIBLIOGRAPHY

This section contains books written for young children and teenagers. Issues of concern to children in stepfamily situations are addressed. This section should be of particular use to teachers and to parents.

There are few books written about stepfamilies for the very young child. It is this author's feeling that this predicament must be remedied quickly. Public awareness of this problem should create more literature for the early childhood level.

288. Adler, C.S. *In Our House Scott Is My Brother*. New York: MacMillan, 1980. Ages 10-15.

A thirteen year old girl tries to adjust to her father's remarriage and to her troublesome stepbrother.

A high interest book that a child will enjoy reading.

289. Beach, C. *Remember Me When I'm Dead*. New York: Elsevier/Nelson, 1980. Ages 13+.

This is the story of two children, Jenny and Sara, who experience strange happenings the first Christmas after their mother's death. A glimpse of their mother's long-vanished friend is followed

by a mysterious letter addressed to their mother
at the place where she had last been seen. A
scrap of mistletoe where their mother always
placed it appears unexplained. Finally, a package
labeled "from Momma" sends the reader into chills.
The new stepmother seems to be the one who is
trying to make Christmas like old-times by refusing
to let past family ties be gone.

290.   Benjamin, Carol Lea. *The Wicked Stepdog*. New
       York: Crowell, 1982. Ages 8-12.

       After her parents get divorced, Louise Branford
       must learn to cope not only with her stepmother,
       but her stepmother's dog as well.

291.   Berger, Terry. *Stepchild*. New York: Julian
       Messner, 1980. Ages 8-12.

       This charming book is about an eleven year old
       stepchild and his new stepfamily. It is written
       in the first person and shows the hero confronting
       issues such as anger, abandonment and disloyalty.
       Each page has a photograph of a real life family
       facing various crises and these pictures help to
       make the book particularly effective.

292.   Berman, Claire. *What Am I Doing in a Stepfamily?*
       Secaucus, N.J.: Lyle Stuart Inc., 1982.
       Illustrated by Dick Wilson. Ages 6-10.

       This is a large print book with colorful illus-
       trations giving advice to children of divorced or
       remarried parents on adjusting to life in a
       stepfamily.

293.   Boeckman, Charles. *Surviving Your Parents'
       Divorce*. New York: Franklin Watts, 1980.
       Ages 10+.

       Chapter 10 gives a positive look into step-
       families. Advice is given to children on dealing
       with their feelings toward new stepfamily members

It can be nice being part of a larger family.
Nobody ever suffered from having more people close
to them in a family circle, people who care about
them. There will be more people with whom to
share your life.

The book as a whole can help children adjust to
their new living style, whether it is in a single
parent home or, if one or both parents remarry,
a home with stepparents, stepbrothers, stepsisters,
or stepgrandparents.

294. Bond, N. *Country of Broken Stone*. New York:
  Atheneum, 1980. Ages 13+.

It is the decision of Penelope's stepmother to
leave the United States and take the family for
the summer to an isolated old stone house in the
north of England so she can continue her profes-
sion as an archaeologist. Penelope has to deal
with the unsettling events of the summer and sort
out the relationships and responsibilities of an
expanded family. She has to cope with trying to
keep peace between her father and her older stepbrother while learning to live in a strange new
home.

295. Booher, Dianna Daniels. *Coping...When Your
  Family Falls Apart*. New York: Julian Messner,
  1982. Ages 13+.

Booher has written a guide for young people
whose parents are in the process of divorcing.
She emphasizes a positive attitude and growth
toward a new life. Chapter Eight deals with the
dating and remarriage of the parents, the instant
stepparent and brothers and sisters.

296. Bradley, Buff. *Where Do I Belong? A Kid's
  Guide to Stepfamilies*. Reading, Mass.: Addison-
  Wesley, 1982. Ages 9-14.

This very optimistic book is about the child's
feelings as a member in the stepfamily. It
emphasizes the special characteristics of stepfamilies. It is a very reassuring book for children

297. Bunting, Eve. *The Big Red Barn*. New York:
      Harcourt Brace Jovanich, 1979. Illustrated
      by Howard Knotts. Ages 5-10.

      A young boy loses his mother and has problems
      accepting his stepmother. His favorite place to
      think and cry burns down, which causes even more
      despair in his life. With his Grandpa's help he
      learns to adjust to new things, while keeping the
      old alive in his heart.

298. Burger, Fredericka. *Nuisance*. New York: Morrow,
      1983. Ages 13+.

      Adjusting to her parents' divorce, her mother's
      remarriage, a new school and neighborhood, Julie
      Howard feels isolated and in the way.

299. Burt, Mala Schuster, and Roger B. Burt. *What's
      Special About Our Stepfamily?* New York: Double-
      day, 1983. Illustrated by Richard Parisi.
      Ages 13+.

      This is the story about some children in a step-
      family. The book is divided into two parts--one
      for children, one for parents. There are places
      in the book for the reader to answer questions
      about his own family as it relates to the family
      in the story. The book has reference pages for
      parents as they go through the book. The section
      for parents is designed to help them understand
      what the children are going through in a divorce/
      remarriage situation.

      This is an excellent book for a restructured
      family to read together.

300. Cherubin, Jan. "Learning to Live With a Step-
        parent." *Seventeen* (April 1983): 97. Ages 13+.

      This is an article dealing with teenagers'
      feelings adjusting to a new stepparent. Tips
      to help the reader feel better about the remar-
      riage are given. A psychologist suggests the
      following: be patient; try to understand your
      own feelings; keep the lines of communication
      open; establish your own space and realize
      parents are people too.

301. Craven, Linda. *Stepfamilies, New Patterns in
        Harmony*. New York: Julian Messner, 1982.
        Ages 13+.

      A book for teenagers dealing with issues such
      as family role conflicts and discipline problems.
      Included is a sensitively handled section on
      sexuality in stepfamilies. Offers practical,
      down-to-earth advice while exploring the special
      problems, feelings and concerns of adolescents
      growing up in a stepfamily.

302. Danziger, Paula. *The Divorce Express*. New York:
        Delacorte, 1982. Ages 13+.

      Fourteen year old Phoebe's divorced mom says
      she is going to marry a man Phoebe cannot abide
      and Phoebe learns that adjusting to change has
      unforeseen rewards.

303. Drescher, Joan. *Your Family, My Family*. New
        York: Walker and Co., 1980. Illustrated by
        Joan Drescher. Ages 13+.

      The book describes different types of families,
      including the stepfamily. It cites some of the
      advantages and strengths of family life.

304. Ewing, Kathryn. *Things Won't Be the Same*.
        New York: Harcout Brace Jovanovich, 1980.
        Ages 10+.

This book is a sequel to *A Private Matter* (1975) about the longing of nine year old Marcy for her own father (she hasn't seen her own father since she was little) and her attachment to an elderly male neighbor.

In this sequel, Marcy is upset by her mother's remarriage and further upset when she learns that she'll be spending some time with her father and stepmother. Realistic portrayal of the difficulty of making adjustments in stepfamilies.

305.   Fields, Terri. "Learning to Live with a Step-
           parent." *Seventeen* (April 1983): 97. Ages 13+.

Written to help teenagers feel happier about and more accepting of their parent's remarriage. Fields interviews many teenagers and their feelings are included in the article. The main theme in the article is that with respect, time, patience and communication, you can learn to live with and ultimately really like one another.

306.   Forman, James. *The Pumpkin Shell*. New York:
           Farrar, Straus and Giroux, 1981. Ages 13+.

Overweight, seventeen year old Robin Flynn finds his once secure life completely turned around by his mother's sudden death, his father's remarriage and his own strong attraction to his beautiful but hostile stepsister.

307.   Gardner, Richard, M.D. *The Boys and Girls
           Book About Stepfamilies*. New York: Bantam Books,
           1982. Ages 6-12.

A warm and honest book that provides reassuring answers to many of the important questions children ask about stepfamilies. The emphasis throughout is on honesty about feelings and on learning to communicate them in appropriate and constructive ways.

308. Gilbert, Sara. *How To Live with a Single Parent*. New York: Lothrop, Lee and Shepard Books, 1982. Ages 7+.

Sara Gilbert talks to young people concerning their confusing feelings about "split" parents. She reveals good times and bad times of single-parent families. Problems, such as money, death, causes of conflict, dating and remarriage, are addressed in simple terms. The final chapter is called "Sources for Support." It provides an excellent bibliography of fiction and non-fiction books for young people. Also included is a list of children's organizations and addresses. There is a separate list of books and organizations for adults.

309. ———. *Trouble At Home*. New York: Lothrop, Lee and Shepard Books, 1981. Ages 13+.

This book is designed primarily for teenagers and is intended to help them cope with changes in a family. The author, in straightforward, commonsense terms, describes frequent family crises, their causes and effects. The chapters dealing with stepfamilies include the disguises of emotion and where, when and how to get help. The emphasis is on understanding and the need to express all feelings. Chapters 8 and 9 (pp. 75-91) are very pertinent.

310. Gould, Robert E., M.D. "How to Survive Your Parents' Divorce." *Seventeen* 6 (June 1983): 114, 115, 141. Ages 13+.

When parents break up, the children should not feel guilty. They should ask questions and parents should take time to explain to the children the reason for the divorce. Before remarriage, the children should be prepared and should be included in the plans.

311. Gregory, D. *There's a Caterpillar in My Lemonade*.
      Reading, Mass.: Addison-Wesley, 1980. Teen-
      agers.

      Samantha has problems coping with her unsettled
      life now that her mother is making plans to re-
      marry. At fourteen, Samantha feels that her life
      is finally settling down and she had just about
      learned to cope with her father's death. Through
      the help of an aunt, Samantha begins to see her
      stepfather not as a caterpillar but a developing
      butterfly. The reader begins to feel that perhaps
      Samantha has grown into a beautiful butterfly
      herself by the mature way she sees her mother's
      relationship with her stepfather.

312. Hazen, Barbara S. *Two Homes to Live In*. New York:
      Human Sciences Press, 1983. Ages 5-8.

313. Helmering, Doris Wild. *I Have Two Families*.
      Nashville: Abingdon, 1981. Illustrated by
      Heidi Palmer. Ages 6-10.

      The story is told by an eight year old girl
      named Patty. She tells about her feelings when
      her mom and dad were divorced. She tells how
      she has two addresses. She lives with her father
      most of the time. She tells how she feels when
      her father goes out on dates and at the end of
      the book she thinks there might be a wedding
      ahead for her father.

314. Hyde, Margaret O. *My Friend Has Four Parents*.
      New York: McGraw-Hill, 1981. Ages 8+.

      Although this book will be found in the
      juvenile literature, it is excellent for parents
      who need the words and information to help their
      children through the transition from divorce to
      remarriage. Hyde makes some insightful statements,
      such as children may feel that the new stepparent
      is going to take the love of their parent away
      and they will lose their only remaining parent.

Also included is some helpful information on
custody trends, parental kidnapping and sources
of outside help.

315. Jackson, Michael, and Jessica Jackson. *Your
      Father's Not Coming Home Anymore*. New York:
      Richard Marek, 1981. Ages 13+.

      A collection of thirty-eight interviews with
      young people between the ages of thirteen and
      twenty-one whose parents have divorced. The
      authors, Michael and Jessica Jackson, were
      eighteen and sixteen at the time of writing and
      are themselves, children of divorced parents.
      Problems with stepparents are a part of many of
      the interviews.

316. Lingard, Joan. *Strangers in the House*. New York:
      Dutton Co., 1983. Ages 13+.

      Fourteen year old Calum and his thirteen year
      old stepsister, Stella, must learn to adjust
      to their parents' marriage, in a story set in
      Scotland.

317. Magid, Ken, and Walt Schreibman. *Divorce Is...
      A Kid's Coloring Book*. Gretna, La.: Pelican
      Press, 1980. Very young children.

318. Martin, Ann M. *Bummer Summer*. New York: Holiday
      House, 1983. Ages 10+.

      Good picture of the early transition to step-
      family living. A twelve year old girl acquires
      a stepmother and two much younger stepsiblings.

319. Mazer, Norma Fox. *Taking Terri Mueller*. New
      York: Avon Books, 1981. Ages 11-15.

      Was it possible to be kidnapped by your own
      father? Fourteen year old Terri remembers only
      life with her father, but then she discovers that
      he kidnapped her from her mother after a divorce
      and that her mother is still alive.

A coloring book for young children illustrated
with scenes and captions regarding the common
dilemmas of children of divorce. There is a
preface for parents.

320. Morgenroth, Barbara. *Will the Real Renie Lake
      Please Stand Up?* New York: Atheneum, 1981.
      Ages 13+.

      Upset over her parents' divorce and her
      father's remarriage, Renie Lake deliberately
      courts trouble. She dabbles in drugs and
      delinquency until a handicapped boy convinces
      her to fight for her future.

321. Noble, June. *Where Do I Fit In?* New York: Holt,
      Rinehart and Winston, 1981. Illustrated by
      Yuri Salzman. Ages 8–10.

      John has a new stepfather. His mother and
      stepfather are expecting a new baby. John is
      beginning to wonder what will become of him when
      this new baby comes. Will his mother still love
      him? He really isn't sure where he fits in this
      family.

      He discovers he fits very well in his new
      stepgrandparents' life. His new stepgrandmother
      makes special goodies for him and his stepgrand-
      father builds a new bait box for him. John decides
      he is pretty lucky. He had three sets of grandpas
      and grandmas who help him feel "at home."

322. Okimoto, Jean Davies. *It's Just Too Much.* New
      York: G.P. Putnam's Sons, 1980. Ages 10–14.

      Cynthia Ann Browne is facing two major changes
      in her life. Cynthia must learn to accept her
      mother's remarriage and her new stepbrothers.
      At the same time, she is faced with the changes
      of puberty and the challenges of junior high
      school. Cynthia meets Seth Rosen, a wonderful
      seventh grader who also has braces. She begins
      to feel that she can take control of her life.

323. Oneal, Libby. *A Formal Feeling*. New York: Viking, 1982. Ages 13+.

Sixteen year old Anne Cameron, home from boarding school for winter vacation, comes to terms with her feelings about her mother's death, her new stepmother and her own place in the world.

324. Oppenheimer, Joan L. *Gardine vs. Hanover*. New York: Crowell, 1982. Ages 13+.

The selfishness and hostility between two teenage stepsisters threatens to destroy the new family that their parents are determined to hold together.

325. Park, Barbara. *Don't Make Me Smile*. New York: Alfred A. Knopf, 1981. Ages 9-12.

Charlie, age eleven, has parents who are getting a divorce. This is the story of how Charlie deals with the divorce, through confusion and then rebellion.

326. Platt, Ken. *Chloris and the Weirdos*. New York: Bantam, 1980. Ages 10-15.

This book is one in which a thirteen year old chronicles life with a mixed-up sister, a twice divorced mother and a boyfriend who is an ace skateboarder.

327. Porterfield, Kay Marie. "Surviving and Thriving with Your Stepparent." *Seventeen* (October 1981). Ages 13+.

"When your mom or dad remarries, you may feel as neglected as Cinderella. With effort and insight, however, you can create a loving, special bond." This article gives suggestions on how to cope with a new stepmother. It tells of what a daughter and stepmother go through to get to know one another. It also lists some tips for easing tension.

328. Randley, Gail. *Nothing Stays the Same Forever*.
      New York: Crown, 1981. Ages 13+.

      Twelve year old Carrie, dismayed at her father's
      impending marriage--only four years after her
      mother's death--and devastated when her friend
      Grace has a heart attack, learns to accept the
      inevitable changes.

329. Robson, Bonnie. *My Parents Are Divorced Too:
      Teenagers Talk About Their Experiences and
      How They Cope*. New York: Everest House, 1980.
      Ages 13+.

      Interviews with twenty-eight young people who
      explore their understanding of their parents'
      divorce, what caused it, their feelings about it
      and how they coped with it. Remarriage issues
      are discussed.

330. Rofes, Eric E. *The Kid's Book of Divorce By,
      For and About Kids*. Lexington, Mass.: The
      Lewis Publishing Co., 1981. Ages 10+.

      This book was written by twenty members, ages
      11-14, of a well known Cambridge school. It is
      an open and practical guide to children's feelings
      about divorce and the issues that children must
      confront during the separation and subsequent
      divorce. Of particular interest is a chapter
      entitled "Stepparents and Other People." In
      this chapter, the children candidly relate
      situations that they have faced and offer the
      reader alternative answers to often encountered
      problems with "Stepparents and Other People."

331. Smith, Doris Buchanan. *The First Hard Times*.
      New York: Viking Press, 1983. Ages 11-15.

      Ancil is a twelve year old girl whose mother
      has remarried since her father has been missing
      in action in Viet Nam for ten years. Ancil's
      struggle with conflicting loyalties is the basis
      of the story. This book would be appropriate
      for a young person adjusting to a new stepparent.

332. Sobol, Harriet Langsam. *My Other Mother, My Other Father*. New York: MacMillan, 1979. Ages 9-12.

Twelve year old Andrea, whose parents have divorced and remarried, discusses the complexities of her new, larger family.

333. Tax, Meredith. *Families*. Boston: Little, Brown, 1981. Illustrated by Marylin Hafner. Ages 6+.

This is a book written for very young children. It describes different kinds of families. Those described include: divorced families, stepmothers, half brothers, large families, families who have adopted children, extended families and one-parent families.

This book would be good for teachers to use when dealing with children who are involved in a divorce or a remarriage.

334. Terris, S. *No Scarlet Ribbons*. New York: Farrar, Straus, Giroux, 1981. Ages 13+.

Rachel is happy about her mother's new marriage and the fact that her junior high English teacher will be her new father. Soon Rachel begins to feel the loss of her closeness with her mother. She attempts to regain her newly married Mom's attention after the rejection she feels when the stepfather and mother want to have some time to themselves. Rachel also gains a brother and sister with her stepfather. At first the idea of a larger family is attractive, but resentment begins to build as her mother shares her time with the new brother and sister. Rachel's stepfather realizes what is happening and when she goes too far and almost destroys the marriage, he comes to her defense and helps Rachel see what she almost lost.

335. Tiersten, Irene. *One Big Happy Family*. New York: St. Martins, 1982. Ages 13+.

Nina Stein leaves her own unsatisfying marriage and moves across town with Daniel, father of two, and they take on the complex demands of work, children, stepchildren, parents, in-laws, ex-spouse and their own relationship.

336. Troyer, Warner. *Divorced Kids*. New York: Harcourt Brace Jovanovich, 1980. Ages 13+.

This book provides a child's view of divorce. The children speak out about their feelings during the divorce. They speak of the pain and bewilderment, lies they were told, the loss of innocence, the coping, the lack of money and the new life with the stepparent. The children give advice to other children on all of these topics. They also speak to mothers, fathers, stepparents and to each other.

Teachers and parents can gain insight into the effects of divorce and family reconstruction on children who are thrust into turmoil against their wills.

337. Vigna, Judith. *She's Not My Real Mother*. Chicago: Albert Whitman and Company, 1980. Ages 5-8.

A young boy finds it very difficult to make friends with his stepmother, because of what his real mother would think. His stepmother takes him to the circus and he gets lost. He was truly happy to see her when he was found. She could never be his real mother, but she could be his friend.

338. ————. *Daddy's New Baby*. Niles, Ill.: Albert Whitman and Co., 1982. Ages 5-8.

A near disaster helps a child of divorced parents soften her feelings toward her father's new baby. Preschool picture book.

339. Westall, R. *The Scarecrows*. New York: Green-
willow, 1981. Ages 13+.

When visiting his mother and stepfather, Simon
suffers a breakdown and is torn by his feelings
of jealousy and betrayal. Simon's mother has
just married an unkempt artist, which is just
the opposite of his dead, soldier father. Simon
hates his new stepfather and becomes enraged
because he believes his stepfather has taken his
mother from him. This is a chilling tale of what
one's imagination can do when hurt and jealousy
dominates one's life.

340. Wolkoff, Judie. *Happily Ever After--Almost*.
Scarsdale, New York: Bradbury, 1982. Ages 13+.

Kitty and Sarah are glad their mother is
marrying Seth, but are uncertain whether they want
to share her with Seth's precocious son.

341. Wright, B. *My New Mom and Me*. Milwaukee: Raintree
Publishers, 1981. Illustrated by Betsy Day.
Ages 6-10.

A preadolescent girl remembers the good and
bad times of her life with her oldest friend, Cat.
She relives the death, funeral and lonely feelings
she and her father shared when her mother died.
After the widower father remarries, she discovers
important new feelings for her stepmother when
Cat disappears and is rescued by the stepmother.
Skillfully written, children can identify with
ways to effectively cope with death and reshaping
a family.

342. Zalben, Jane Breskin. *Maybe It Will Rain*
Tomorrow. New York: Farrar, Straus, Giroux,
1982. Ages 13+.

After her mother's suicide, seventeen year
old Beth Corey must move in with her father and
his new family and discovers that she must learn
to depend upon herself.

AUDIO-VISUAL RESOURCES

The audio-visual materials listed below are given as an additional resource for readers of this book. Because there are so few available resources, older films are included.

CBS Magazine on Stepfamilies. 13 minutes. Distributor: Stepfamily Foundation, Inc., 333 West End Ave., New York, N.Y. 10023. This video tape portrays a number of step situations.

Complete Set of 1983 Annual Conference Workshops. Set of 17 tapes. Distributor: Stepfamily Association of America, Inc., Sales Program, 28 Allegheny Ave., Suite 1307, Towson, Md. 21204. Includes guest speakers, David and Vera Mace.

Daddy Doesn't Live Here Anymore: The Single-Parent Family. 52 minutes, color. Written by Robert Weiss. Distributor: Human Relations Media, 175 Tompkins Avenue, Pleasantville, N.Y. 10570. Four parts of the filmstrip include: The Changing Family, When Parents Divorce, One Day at a Time and The Stepfather Family.

Family Enrichment. Set of two tapes, 1983. Written by David and Vera Mace. Distributor: Stepfamily Association of America, Inc., Sales Program, 28 Allegheny Ave., Suite 1307, Towson, Md. 21204. Taken from 1983 annual membership conference of SAA.

*I Have Some Good News and Some Bad News! What Is
   Expectable in a Stepfamily.* Set of two tapes,
   1983. By workshop leader Mary Jean Weston.
   Distributor: Stepfamily Association of America,
   Inc., Sales Program, 28 Allegheny Ave., Suite 1307,
   Towson, Md. 21204.

Instant Love: Exploring the Stepfamily Myth. One tape,
   1983. By workshop leader Elizabeth Einstein.
   Distributor: Stepfamily Association of America,
   Inc., Sales Program, 28 Allegheny Ave., Suite 1307,
   Towson, Md. 21204.

Living in Step for the Woman Who Has Never Parented.
   30 minutes. Distributor: Stepfamily Foundation,
   Inc., 333 West End Ave., New York, N.Y. 10023.

Making Father Custody Families Work. Set of two tapes,
   1983. By workshop leader Roger Burt. Distributor:
   Stepfamily Association of America, Inc., Sales
   Program, 28 Allegheny Ave., Suite 1307, Towson, Md.
   21204. Unedited tape of workshop given at 1983
   annual membership conference of SAA.

Me and Dad's New Wife. 33 minutes, color, 1976.
   Producer: David Wilson. Starring Kristy McNichol.
   Based on *A Smart Kid Like You* by Stella Peusner.
   Distributor: Time-Life Video Distribution Center,
   100 Eisenhower, Paramus, N.J. 07652.

Non-Custodial Parenting. Set of two tapes, 1983. By
   workshop leader Jess Young. Distributor: Stepfamily
   Association of America, Inc., Sales Program, 28
   Allegheny Ave., Suite 1307, Towson, Md. 21204.
   Unedited tape of workshop given at 1983 annual
   membership conference of SAA.

October 1983 Professional Seminar. Series of six audio
   tapes. Distributor: Stepfamily Foundation, Inc.,
   333 West End Ave., New York, N.Y. 10023. Unedited
   version of complete Stepfamily Foundation Professional Seminar held on October 21-22, 1983.

Parenting and Stepparenting in Stepfamilies. By workshop leader Helen Coale Lewis. Set of two tapes, 1983. Distributor: Stepfamily Association of America, Inc., Sales Program, 28 Allegheny Ave., Suite 1307, Towson, Md. 21204. Unedited tape of workshop given at 1983 annual membership conference of SAA.

Professional Seminar. 6 hours. Distributor: Stepfamily Foundation, Inc., 333 West End Ave., New York, N.Y. 10023. Unedited version of a recent Stepfamily Foundation Professional Seminar.

Sex Education in Stepfamilies: A Must! By workshop leaders Claire Berman and John Visher. Set of two tapes. Distributor: Stepfamily Association of America, Inc., Sales Program, 28 Allegheny Ave., Suite 1307, Towson, Md. 21204. Unedited tape of workshop given at 1983 annual membership conference of SAA.

Special Tape Series. 210 minutes (30 minutes each tape). Distributor: Stepfamily Foundation, Inc., 333 West End Ave., New York, N.Y. 10033. Discussion presented by Jeannette Lofas on specific areas of stepfamily relationships: (1) children and remarriage; (2) discipline; (3) the couple; (4) structuring the family; (5) the prior spouse; (6) before marriage; (7) stepfamily foundation tools and processes for couples and families.

Stepparenting Issues. 20 minutes, color, 13 vignettes. Distributor: Family Service Association of America, 44 East 23rd Street, New York, N.Y. 10010. Situations experienced by members of remarried family include: no time alone for the new couple; conflicts over child rearing; children testing a stepparent's authority; children exploiting the differences between the former spouse and new spouse and sibling rivalry.

Stepparenting. Distributor: American Personnel and
    Guidance Association, Order Services Dept. #F11,
    Two Skyline Place, Suite 400, 5203 Leesburg Pike,
    Falls Church, Va. 22041.

Stepparenting: New Families, Old Ties. 25 minutes,
    color, 1977. Distributor: Polymorph Films, 118
    South Street, Boston, Mass. 02115. Stepparents
    in this film discuss their feelings about their
    new roles. Members of a stepparent support group
    talk about specific situations. Contains documen-
    tary scenes of stepfamily life. Decisions about
    having more children is also discussed.

    Interesting film that provides excellent background
    information for those who work with children or
    parents from stepfamilies.

Stepteens Tell It Like It Is...For Them! Set of two
    tapes, 1983. By workshop leaders Marilyn and
    Cecil Wyman. Distributor: Stepfamily Association
    of America, Inc., Sales Program, 28 Allegheny Ave.,
    Suite 1307, Towson, Md. 21204. Taken from 1983
    annual membership conference of SAA.

The Dynamics of Step. 30 minutes. By Jeannette Lofas
    and Ruth Roosevelt. Distributor: Stepfamily
    Foundation, Inc., 333 West End Ave., New York,
    N.Y. 10023. The co-authors of *Living In Step*,
    Lofas and Roosevelt, discuss the special dynamics
    of step relationships and the work of the Step-
    family Foundation.

The Syndromes, Dynamics and Issues. 12 minutes.
    Produced by: NBC using people from Stepfamily
    Foundation. Distributor: Stepfamily Foundation,
    Inc., 333 West End Ave., New York, N.Y. 10023.

Teenagers in Stepfamilies: Trials and Joys. Set of
    two tapes, 1983. By workshop leader Ann L. Getzoff.
    Distributor: Stepfamily Association of America,
    Inc., Sales Program, 28 Allegheny Ave., Suite 1307,
    Towson, Md., 21204. Unedited tape of workshops
    given at the 1983 annual membership conference
    of SAA.

Video Tapes for Professionals. 1 hour. Distributor: Stepfamily Foundation, Inc., 333 West End Ave., New York, N.Y. 10023. Edited excerpts of Jeannette Lofas teaching professionals the specific dynamics of "step."

ORGANIZATIONAL RESOURCES

The organizations listed in this section offer information about programs, newsletters and support services for families involved in a stepfamily situation. Some organizations are clearinghouses for information or could help one find a therapist.

To find local services, parents should consult agencies serving families, such as community health centers, family service or youth service of the local city or county, or child guidance centers. Clergy or family counselors can refer parents locally for specific services related to remarriage. A listing of sources is included in the yellow pages of telephone directories under lawyers, marriage and family counseling, psychologists and psychotherapists.

American Association of Marriage and Family Therapists, 225 Yale Ave., Claremont, CA 91711.

American Psychiatric Association, 1700 18th Street, N.W., Washington, D.C. 20009.

For help in finding a therapist.

American Psychological Association, 1200 17th Street, N.W., Washington, D.C. 20036.

American Society for Adolescent Psychiatry, 24 Green Valley Road, Wallingford, PA 19086.

For help in finding a therapist.

Center for the Family in Transition, 5725 Paradise
   Drive, Corte Madera, CA 94925.

   The center is a non-profit agency funded by private
   foundation monies to bring together a wide range
   of clinical, research and educational programs
   (i.e., "The Visiting Game") for and on behalf of
   children in families undergoing separation, divorce
   or remarriage.

Center for Parenting Studies, Wheelock College, 200
   The Riverway, Boston, MA 02215.

   For publications and seminars on parenting for
   professionals and parents.

Divorce Resource and Mediation Center, Inc., 2464
   Massachusettes Ave., Cambridge, MA 02140.

   Provides support groups, individual and group
   therapy, mediation and marriage and remarriage
   counseling. Serves New England region.

The Family Center, 210 California Ave., Suite 6, Palo
   Alto, CA 94306.

   Parent groups and mediation counseling.

The Family Education Center of Florida, P.O. Box 260421,
   Tampa, FL 33685.

   The center's function is educational in nature and
   offers workshops for parents on stepfamily living.

Family Resources/Referral Center, National Council on
   Family Relations, 1219 University Ave., S.E.,
   Minneapolis, MN 55414.

Family Service Association of America, 44 East 23rd
   Street, New York, NY 10010.

   For guidance in finding the right kind of assistance
   in local areas.

Listening Incorporated, Gary, IN 46403.

>   Co-founded by Richard and Patricia Bennett. Pro-
vides counseling workshops and newsletters to stepfamilies.

National Association of Social Workers, 1425 H Street,
N.W., Suite 600, Washington, D.C. 20005.

>   For help in finding a therapist.

National Council on Family Relations.

>   Have annual meetings where current research is
presented.

National Institute of Mental Health, Public Inquiries,
5600 Fishers Lane, Rockville, MD 20857.

>   Ask for: Duffin, S. *Yours, Mine and Ours: Tips
for Stepparents*. DHEW Pub. No. (ADM) 78-676 (1978).

>>   Espinoza R., and Y. Newman, *Stepparenting*.
DHEW Pub. No. (ADM) 78-579 (1979).

National Registry of Clinical Social Workers, 7981
Eastern Ave., Silver Spring, MD 20910.

Parents Without Partners.

>   Sponsors "Education for Remarriage" groups in
some cities.

Remarried Incorporate, Box 742, Santa Ana, CA 92701.

>   For information about programs for stepfamilies
that may be social, educational or cultural in
nature.

Second Wives Association of North America (SWAN), Box
978, Station F, Toronto, Ontario, Canada M4Y2N9.

An informational and support group open to second
wives and their husbands. Offers a chance for
couples to talk out issues that arise in second
marriages.

Stepfamily Association of America, Inc. 28 Allegheny
Ave., Suite 1307, Towson, MD 21204.

The association is a non-profit organization that
acts as a support network and national advocate
for stepparents, remarried parents, and their
children. The association offers memberships, a
quarterly bulletin, informational materials,
annual conferences, books and other publications,
public information, workshops, professional
training and research.

The Step Family Foundation, 333 West End Avenue, New
York, NY 10023.

Clearinghouse of information and research on stepfamilies.

U.S. Department of Health, Education and Welfare.

Ask for: No. 74-1903: R.P. Kuhn, and K.M. Williams,
Remarriages, Rockville, MD.

Stepparent's Forum, Westmount, P.O. Box 4002, Montreal,
H3I2X3, Canada.

Periodical designed to offer support and guidance
to stepparents.

NEWSLETTERS

Effective Parenting. American Guidance Service, Publishers Building, Circle Pines, Minnesota 55014.

Newsletter for sponsors of parent training.

The Family Therapy Networker. 2334 Cedar Lane, Vienna, Virginia 22180.

Remarriage. G & R Publications, Inc., 648 Beacon Street, Boston, Massachusetts 02215.

Monthly newsletter that provides insight, guidance, and legal advice for remarried couples.

Stepparent News. Listening Inc., 8716 Pine Ave., Gary, Indiana 46403.

Newsletter for parents and professionals.

Stepfamily Bulletin. $4.50 yearly. Stepfamily Association of America, Inc., 28 Allegheny Ave., Suite 1307, Towson, Maryland 21204.

1981: Nos. 1, 2, 3, 4.
1982: Nos. 1, 2, 3 & 4 combined.
1983: Nos. 1, 2, 3, 4.

U.S. Bureau of the Census, Current Population Reports. In the past has published:
(a) Marriage, Divorce, Widowhood and Remarriage: 1967, Series P-20, No. 312, 1977.

111

    (b) Marital Status and Living Arrangements,
        Series P-20, No. 349, 1979.
    (c) American Families and Living Arrangements,
        Series P-23, No. 104, 1979.

INDEX